**Pra**

"I enjoyed reading this book so much; Kristin has a beautiful way of weaving powerful Scripture with everyday, practical life. She adds thoughts and application to stories and passages I've heard many times, but her unique take on them reminds us that our ultimate goal is to have priorities that reflect Jesus. I love the fact that she's honest and forthcoming about her own struggles and frustrations and I felt invited into her life and her wrestling as a sister who feels the same. I'd recommend this to any woman trying to free herself from the distractions of this world in order to live a more peaceful, focused, and God-centered life as the woman Jesus created her to be."

—**Angie Smith**, nationally recognized Bible teacher and best-selling author of *Seamless: Understanding The Bible as One Complete Story, Chasing God*, and *What Women Fear*

"Just when a mama thinks she's going under with mothering (which includes All. The. Things.), Kristin Funston leads us to more. With a girlfriend-in-the-trenches voice, she shows us how to grow our souls while our kids are still growing."

—**Amy Carroll**, Proverbs 31 Ministries speaker and writer, author of *Breaking Up with Perfect* and *Exhale*

"If you are a mom who feels tired, worn out, or a bit flustered with all you've got to get done, Kristin has a word for you! In *More for Mom*, Kristin makes us laugh and get serious all in the same paragraph. She boldly shares the truth but makes sure we know she's right there with us as she leads us to the one thing we need to live a more whole and holy life as a mom—Jesus."

—**Micah Maddox**, women's conference speaker and author of *Anchored In: Experience a Power-Full Life in a Problem-Filled World*

"How is life? Read this book and it may change your answer. I work with Kristin at our church so I can tell you she is real, she is honest, and she is not just writing words on a page. Like you, she has a full life, but she is willing to ask honest questions and share honest answers. Take a journey with Kristin through this book and learn what it means to experience a completely abundant and whole life."

—**Mary Ann Ruff**, Executive Director & Director of Women's Ministry, Hope Church, Memphis

"Kristin Funston is the best friend all hard-working mommas need in their corner. Her fun approach unmasks the things we feel on a daily basis—unrelenting mom guilt. Instead of doing more and adding more to our already full plates, my friend encourages us to receive more of what we need from Jesus. It's time for us to ask for more without hesitation from our Heavenly Father who longs to give us everything we need in life. When we feel like we are supposed to be doing more and be more, Kristin shows us that Jesus is the more we are looking for to help us live our whole and holy life."

—**Jennifer Renee Watson**, speaker and author of *Freedom!: The Gutsy Pursuit of Breakthrough and the Life Beyond It*

"Frazzled moms, do you realize you are worth far more than the piles of laundry and homework and deadlines you're hiding under? You most certainly will by the time you've finished this beautiful book. Reading *More for Mom* is like hanging out with a dear friend who sees your real and messy life and loves you all the more for it. Yet she cares enough not to let you wallow there. With her signature humor, candor, and wisdom, Kristin Funston shows us how we really can grasp the abundant life God offers us—right where we are."

—**Becky Kopitzke**, author of *Generous Love: Discover the Joy of Living "Others First"* and *The SuperMom Myth: Conquering the Dirty Villains of Motherhood*

"Do you view the spiritual disciplines as daunting items to check off your list and get right? I sure did, until Kristin helped me realize that God uses them to give us more—not more pressures and demands on our time but more strength and more peace. As a busy mom, I'm relieved that God isn't out to deplete us with added stress but desires to equip us for godly success. Here's to more life, through Christ!"

—**Katie M. Reid**, mom to five and author of *Made Like Martha: Good News for the Woman Who Gets Things Done*

"All moms know that life can be exhausting and overwhelming, but Kristin Funston provides a new way forward in *More for Mom*. With sincerity and grace, Kristin illuminates a new way to see the good, beautiful, and holy life offered to all moms. Practical and helpful!"

—**Nicole Unice**, Discipleship Pastor, Hope Church, Richmond, VA; author of *The Struggle Is Real*

"Kristin Funston has great news for mothers who want to live a whole, holy life. In her book, *More for Mom*, she offers practical steps to throw off the performance metrics by learning how to listen and ask God for His assignment for your life. Kristin infuses hope in the heart of every mother. This book will start you thinking about how to apply scripture to everyday situations as you wisely navigate every decision. With biblical wisdom and common sense, Kristin encourages you to embrace the high calling of motherhood. You will find help and practical ideas through the pages of this book."

—**Connie Albers**, speaker and author of *Parenting Beyond the Rules*

"Using the perfect blend of humor and solid biblical teaching, Kristin does a fantastic job of pointing weary moms to the MORE that is available to us in Jesus Christ. She is clearly gifted at breaking down Scripture to make it more understandable and applicable for her readers and even helped me see some very familiar passages with fresh eyes! Reading *More for Mom* feels like having the BEST conversation with a wise and trusted friend."

—**Amy Hale**, Bible teacher, speaker, online influencer

Kristin Funston

More ~~from~~ for Mom

Living
Your Whole
and Holy
Life

Abingdon Press
Nashville

**Library of Congress Cataloging-in-Publication Data**

Names: Funston, Kristin, author.
Title: More for mom : living your whole & holy life / Kristin Funston.
Description: Nashville : Abingdon Press, [2019] | Includes bibliographical references
Identifiers: LCCN 2018053532 (print) | LCCN 2019003481 (ebook) | ISBN
  9781501879722 (ebook) | ISBN 9781501879715 (pbk. : alk. paper)
Subjects: LCSH: Motherhood—Religious aspects—Christianity. | Mothers—Religious life.
Classification: LCC BV4529.18 (ebook) | LCC BV4529.18 .F86 2019 (print) | DDC
  248.8/431—dc23
LC record available at https://urldefense.proofpoint.com/v2/url?u=https-3A__lccn.loc.gov_
2018053532&d=DwIFAg&c=_GnokDXYZpxapTjbCjzmOH7Lm2x2J46Ijwz6YxXCKeo&r=
ox0wiE5wyqlD4NWBvXI_LEW57Ah1_xv-dTElReAYRyw&m=FTrrJiUsSD-2S35B6uUaKKl
2md_2K1IEgqozAV064WM&s=w3CKd8GnDx9yiMxfUYgbLItfjY2ClJFQKaIAgwcUKis&e=

19 20 21 22 23 24 25 26 27—10 9 8 7 6 5 4 3 2 1

MANUFACTURED IN THE UNITED STATES OF AMERICA

*To Bryant, McKenna, Meda, and Rockie May.*
*I love you more. I love you the most.*
*I love you the most-est in the whole wide world.*

*To my Hope Church family. You brought this unchurched girl to church.*

*To you, who—like me—are literally living on a prayer. And lukewarm coffee.*
*And the occasional glass of wine. You are so loved.*

# Contents

A Quick Note to My Friend . . . . . . . . . . . . . . . . . . . . . . . . . . . . . . . . . . . xi

Part 1: Whole and Holy Mom . . . . . . . . . . . . . . . . . . . . . . . . . . 1

   1. The Whole Enchilada. . . . . . . . . . . . . . . . . . . . . . . . . . . . . . . . . 3
   2. Holy Moly . . . . . . . . . . . . . . . . . . . . . . . . . . . . . . . . . . . . . . . . . . 23

Part 2: Living This Mom Life . . . . . . . . . . . . . . . . . . . . . . . . . 43

   3. Playing Games . . . . . . . . . . . . . . . . . . . . . . . . . . . . . . . . . . . . . 45
   4. Holier Than Thou . . . . . . . . . . . . . . . . . . . . . . . . . . . . . . . . . 64
   5. Raving Fans. . . . . . . . . . . . . . . . . . . . . . . . . . . . . . . . . . . . . . . 82
   6. Blinders On. . . . . . . . . . . . . . . . . . . . . . . . . . . . . . . . . . . . . . 101
   7. Come Alive . . . . . . . . . . . . . . . . . . . . . . . . . . . . . . . . . . . . . . 118

Part 3: More for Mom . . . . . . . . . . . . . . . . . . . . . . . . . . . . . . . 139

   8. More Time . . . . . . . . . . . . . . . . . . . . . . . . . . . . . . . . . . . . . . 141
   9. More Fasting. . . . . . . . . . . . . . . . . . . . . . . . . . . . . . . . . . . . . 162
   10. More Life. . . . . . . . . . . . . . . . . . . . . . . . . . . . . . . . . . . . . . . 184

Invitation to Be Whole and Holy . . . . . . . . . . . . . . . . . . . . . . . 204
Acknowledgments. . . . . . . . . . . . . . . . . . . . . . . . . . . . . . . . . . . . . 207

# A Quick Note to My Friend

*H*eeeyyyy! I am so, so glad you are here.

It may seem like you picked up this book on a whim or like this book just happened about out of nowhere. Maybe you're standing in the bookstore and saw this awesomely peaceful-looking cover—if I do say so myself—and read the title and thought, *Wait— more* for *me? I'm intrigued. Let me take a look.*

Maybe you are online shopping during your lunch break, trying to find a gift for your BFF, and this is the top option. Go ahead; click purchase. It's a *great* gift for your girlfriend.

Years of energy, thought, and prayer have gone into the pages that follow, along with real-life experience. The experience you probably know so well—the give, give, give of motherhood that leaves us exhausted and often physically, emotionally, and spiritually depleted because—*man, oh man*—kids. Maybe your own children are still in diapers or just beginning to experience the terrifying world of puberty, or maybe they're driving off to high school, college, or their first job. Wherever you are in your motherhood journey, I know you're a giver. That's what mothers are. We give and give and give, right?

I feel like we're friends already. Like we're sitting down to finally catch up after a long season of crazy. A long season of sleepless nights, busy days, long work hours, and a lot of responsibilities and others' expectations to manage.

But here we are, ready to meet up with each other and Jesus. Maybe through these pages we're meeting in a coffee shop or bookstore, in your comfy living room recliner, or maybe we're even in the car line together picking up your kids from school—because life don't stop, yo.

I can't wait for you to join me in this journey of learning how to live our whole and holy lives. And it's going to be a journey. We'll talk about some hard stuff, some easy stuff, even some goofy and totally random stuff.

But it's all *good* stuff. It's stuff that stems from a good, holy, and almighty God who doesn't need anything *from* us to make our worlds go 'round. It's stuff that when flipped on its head shows us our God has more *for* us.

Scripture tells us in Job 12 that "in His hand is the life of *every* living thing / and the breath of *all* mankind" (v. 10, emphasis mine). He is the God who gives everything to us—from the breath we breathe to the paychecks we cash, from the homes we live in to the feelings tugging at our hearts. He is the God who gives plentifully, so much so that what He gives can't be contained. Scripture backs this up throughout history. We also know according to Ephesians 3:20 that He "is able to do far more abundantly" than we could *even think* or *ask*! This is because His power at work inside us never ends.

Limitless giving can be so hard to imagine on this side of heaven, right? Especially because our daily grind begs *us* to keep giving and giving. Kids, dinner, homework, conference calls, softball and football practices, the PTA, the board of directors, spouses, parents, even siblings—each day brings another round of giving of our time, energy, thoughts, love, and emotional and physical strength. And money. Don't forget the money.

Don't get me wrong; these are all great to give ourselves to. But I'm ready for us to give from a place of abundance where we can do more than just give; we can give in a celebratory way because we've *already* received more than *would ever* be enough. This perspective will shape what our daily grind looks and feels like because we'll finally recognize what it means to be whole and holy in the day-to-day.

Our individualistic and fast-paced culture tugs hard at us to keep on looking out for number one, but as believers, we simultaneously know that Christ desires for us to rely on Him. His timeless spiritual disciplines—such as fasting, prayer, and prioritizing time for Him— are obvious yet extremely underused strategies for getting more out of this life He has blessed us with. So we're going to go back to the basics with some of them in order to bring back space for more of Christ in our modern times.

In our journey through these pages, we'll chat about the mental games we often play and how to *recognize* and *strategize* a game plan for the times our minds—and Satan—try to win us over. This journey will also help reveal hidden truths about relationships and expectations we hold. Truths that will set us free from chains we didn't even know were binding us.

We're even taking the extra steps to learn how to make our hopes, dreams, and passions a part of our reality.

All of this together will empower each of us to start living our already whole and holy life in Christ. Because it's there already—just waiting. And it's more than we can even begin to imagine.

I can't wait for us to start believing God for more in this crazy-busy work, home, married or single-mom life we've got going on.

**And I can't wait for all of us—all the moms of our**

**generation—to stop believing the lie that more is needed *from* us and start living the truth that more is available *for* us.**

When I first sat down to write this to you, I got the overwhelming feeling that Jesus wanted us to know that *this*—the ride and awakening process throughout this book—is going to be fun. Fun for Him to watch and for us to live. Fun despite the hectic days, despite the screaming kids, despite the anxiety and overload of our stretched-too-thin lives.

I know and He knows that, in our reality as modern-day, work-hard mamas, a lot is expected from us daily. We're *moms* after all. We basically run the world.

But we can still have fun, despite all of this. I'm always down to have fun, so I say let's do this together.

Much love,
Kristin

# Whole and Holy Mom

PART 1

# The Whole Enchilada

And God saw everything that he had made, and
behold, it was very good. (Genesis 1:31)

Everywhere I turn women—friends, family, neighbors, coworkers, church members—are talking about the busyness of their lives and how, no matter what strategies they employ, they can't seem to get on top of it all.

I'm willing to bet it's the same with you and your friends too.

Whether you call yourself a stay-at-home mom; a working mom; a boy mom; a girl mom; a caffeinated mom; a purple, blue, or yellow mom; or a *whatever* mom, work-hard mamas are everywhere. Although the moms look different than they used to look, most tend to be responsible for more than what's inside the walls of their home, more than dinner on the table and tending the children.

A 2016 study showed that "69.9 percent of mothers with children under age 18 were in the labor force, representing over a third (34.2 percent) of working women."[1] So stand with two other mom friends of yours, and the odds are that one or two of you are what most call "working moms."

Can I be frank with you? The term "working mom" confuses me.

Because what mother *isn't* working? It seems ridiculously redundant. Though for the sake of our conversation here, we'll consider anyone with children and obligations beyond her home and family—paid or not—to be a working mom or, better yet, a work-hard mama.

So do you work full- or part-time for a large company or yourself *and* have full or shared responsibility for children in your home? Do you stay at home with your children during the day? Do you work from a home office or in a cubicle? Do you get a regular paycheck or volunteer your time for zero monetary payment? Do you work hard to keep your family safe, fed, and healthy each and every day?

If the answer is yes to any of these questions, you are welcome and safe here. You have a whole lot going on in your life, right?! You are a work-hard, modern mama.

> *Who else is too tired for big plans? (And all the mamas of infants and toddlers raised their hands.) While the idea of "big plans" is exciting, I'm too exhausted and worn thin to hear what they are, let alone do them.*

I am too, and we are in this together. I have been in each of the scenarios listed above. I have worked forty-plus hours a week, both inside *and* outside the home. I have also been a part-time employee, splitting time between a remote office and an in-home office—all while being a mother. I even spent a short stint as a stay-at-home mom until we ran out of money and I ran out of sanity. But even then, I was still always working.

I am here to tell you something, although I venture to guess you already know what I'm about to say. None of the differences in the amount, place, or kind of work matter. Not one. Moms who work day in and day out—at home, in an office, in their cars, forty hours a week, fifteen hours a week—*all* feel there's something incomplete about their lives, and most are in need of a spiritual reset. They feel far from living the holy life they think they are supposed to live. They think whole is for someone who has all the pieces of her life figured out and placed neatly together. They think holy is for someone who prays or sings worship songs all day long or who remembers to teach her kids how to pray eloquent psalms.

You probably know what I'm talking about.

> *It's being content in the crazy and having*
> *peace knowing that God's in control, even*
> *when I'm stretched thin and don't feel like I*
> *can do anything else.*

It's the mixture of emotions, expectations, and our people all yanking on us while yelling so loud we can't hear ourselves think. And more important—and more *unfortunately*—it's the fear and dread that we aren't living up to or doing what we believe to be God's will for our lives because we're so busy managing the day-to-day details.

If allowed, the daily grind can suck the life right out of us, leaving us too exhausted to live up to our godly potential. But the Bible tells us we can "do all things through him who strengthens me" (Philippians 4:13).

Yep. I just did it. I threw out a heavy Bible verse only a few pages into our time together. You should know that I think this verse is great, but gosh, sometimes I feel like I cannot do more than merely survive, let alone live up to huge expectations that God—or anybody else!—has for me. You with me?

Jeremiah 29:11 says He has plans for us—for you and for me—and they are big plans.

But who else is too tired for big plans? (And all the mamas of infants and toddlers raised their hands.)

While the idea of "big plans" is exciting, I'm too exhausted and worn thin to hear what they are, let alone *do* them.

> *Each of us is a whole person with one whole life, and we were designed to experience the holy of this life now, on earth.*

This is a breaking point for me, and I dare say it is for you as well. How do we live the holy life Jesus brought to us? How do we live as whole women when our lives seem fragmented? I want to know how to balance being a work-hard mom on a scale tipping heavily back and forth, one side always heavier than the other. What about you?

If we look back at Philippians 4:13, where Paul said, "I can do all things through him who strengthens me," we may want to also look at a few of the preceding verses in order to move on in this journey.

> Not that I am speaking of being in need, for I have learned in whatever situation I am to be content. I know how to be brought low, and I know how to abound. In any and every circumstance, I have learned the secret of facing plenty and hunger, abundance and need. I can do all things through him who strengthens me.
> (Philippians 4:11-13)

We sometimes tend to latch on to this idea of doing, which Paul throws out in our favorite verse 13, as a catchall for dreaming big, doing the thing, and doing it well. But if we read the verse in context, we see that Paul is more likely saying we can *endure* all things through Christ.

It's being content in the crazy and having peace knowing that God's in control, even when I'm stretched thin and don't feel like I can do anything else.

It sounds easier than it is, right? Where does this contentment and peace come from?

Well, it comes in the recognition that we are not pieces and parts, that we can move toward a whole, and therefore holy, life. **Each of us is a whole person with one whole life, and we were designed to experience the holy of this life now, on earth.**

It's funny how we get swept up into whatever is happening in our work life or mom life or social life, often without thinking of how one ripples the tides of another.

But our lives shouldn't be compartmentalized like this. All of the parts Jesus has given us to live allow us to move toward the *one* life He planned for us in the beginning.

Without Him, we merely give pieces to what could be a complete and abundantly WHOLE life.

I don't know about you, but in this game of life, I want to win big. I want the whole enchilada. Do you?

## My Portfolio Life

In his book *The Art of Work,* Jeff Goins used the term "portfolio lifestyle" to describe how Americans live. My Type-A self loves this picture.

When I hear the word *portfolio,* I think of a briefcase or folder with organized documents and examples showcasing our best work. The achiever in me adores the idea of a neat, tidy, organized life, showing only my best work.

However, when I looked up the word *portfolio,* words such as *range* and *varied* fell under the definition. It even mentioned "loose sheets," which made me both laugh and nod my head in agreement in regard to the "loose and random" information filling my brain at any given moment.

As moms, we can very easily use these terms to describe our day-to-day lives. Activities such as changing diapers or cleaning toilets vary widely from conference calls or opportunity reports on profit and loss. Our lives are filled with "loose sheets" of soccer team contact information, sales projections, grocery lists, and mortgage due dates.

There is a lot to keep up with. Am I right or *amiright*?

*He has given us vocations, relationships, friends, family, and* Him *to steer us toward a whole life. These necessarily impact one another and shouldn't be compartmentalized.*

Sure, there are contrasts in the day-to-day details of each of our situations. My crazy is going to look different from yours, but the level on which that craziness and the demands on our individual lives functions is the same. All work-hard mamas deal with emotional and physical hardship.

OK, let me clarify. Having children brings on the emotional and physical hardship. But I would never blame our beloved children for complicating our lives. *Never.*

Currently, I work part-time from home and part-time in an office. My days are spent running carpools, driving to preschool drop-offs, sitting outside art and gymnastics lessons, and supporting my cyclist husband at races. Simultaneously, I'm writing articles, supervising homework, building websites, running social media campaigns, emailing invoices, teaching classes, and cooking dinner poorly, cleaning up after four—yes, *four*!—smelly pets, not including the eight chickens that recently moved into our suburban-farm backyard.

In the nine years I have been a parent, my life has become an overflowing bucket of random. Besides dealing with the kiddos 657 hours a day—I assure you, logging that number of hours in a day feels possible in my house so I am assuming it does in yours too—I have not even mentioned volunteering through church, small group gatherings, and other obligations I have added to the chaos. Needless to say, things are busy. Please tell me this sounds vaguely familiar.

I bet your life is pretty similar in the grand scheme of things, or you probably would not have opened this book.

Don't get me wrong; chaos is not necessarily a bad thing if handled correctly, because it offers growth and opportunities to stretch us. But chaos is hard. It is hard to juggle and package neatly into our box of life. And oftentimes, this juggling act can be a painful one.

The thing that's interesting about this "portfolio" idea is that all the randomness, all those loose and varied sheets together, create one *single* portfolio, one all-encompassing briefcase that portrays our work.

Guess what all this randomness and the messy details of our daily lives make up. Our *one* life that God has packaged together into one *whole* life. And from here on out, we're going to work to make our portfolios portray *complete* lives from what God has provided through Jesus Christ. Ready to see your life as not merely pieces but a complete picture?

Would you join me in beginning to believe we *can* live a whole and holy life even though we're bone tired? That we *can* believe God for more, even though we're stretched thin across all the pieces of our working-mom life?

He has given us vocations, relationships, friends, family, and

*Him* to steer us toward a whole life. These necessarily impact one another and shouldn't be compartmentalized.

Believing that we can live whole lives will lead to transformation for you and me, from the inside out. I know Jesus is waiting to hand us the prize at the end of this life. He's waiting to give us all of it—the whole enchilada.

Our lives are full, but are they whole? Do we offer our whole selves to our people and our God rather than leftovers from the day or week?

If the answer is no—if our lives are not whole—then something's got to give.

## It's Time for a Change

It's changed millions of lives, leading to transformation inside and out, in both form and appearance. Nobody claimed it was easy, but millions of people have completed the program and changed their lives because of it.

I'm talking about the Whole30 program, of course. By removing sugar, alcohol, grains, legumes, soy, and dairy, people have cleansed their bodies and drastically altered all areas of their lives.

> *Even if you are overworked and over capacity,*
> *you can still ask for more. In fact, I say you*
> *must ask for more. More for us instead of*
> *from us.*

Now before you go on assuming I am one of these millions who are changed, don't. I love my soy sauce, beans, rice, and honey-drizzled baked brie too much to ever cut them out completely. Bring on the cheese, please!

So I'm not here to talk about dairy, soy, and diets, but I *am* here to talk about change, a change that steps us into a more whole and holy life. It leads to inside-and-out transformation. But this change doesn't start with a physical reset the way Whole30 or any of the other trendy diet plans pushed these days do. I'm talking about a complete spiritual change. And I believe busy moms are often the ones most in need of a reset. Can I get an amen?

Whole30 followers achieve a physical reset by eating only whole and complete unprocessed foods. What if, instead of working to be whole and healthy physically, we worked toward becoming whole spiritually, even holy, focusing on changing our relationship with God and other people in the same way we focus on what we eat? And what if we found more nourishment for the daily grind instead of feeling depleted, as relationships and effort normally make us feel.

Just as Whole30 focuses on what foods to eliminate in order to reset a person's physical bodies, we need to look at how we're living, what we are consuming and not consuming, to live how God intended for us to live. I believe we must consume only whole and holy thoughts and actions to spiritually reset. Only the thoughts from His voice, not man's.

This begins with asking God for more.

Join me in a collective groan right here. *More?*

Most of us are scared, hesitant, and even downright adamant about not asking for more on our plate. What possibly do we have time to add?

But even if you are overworked and over capacity, you can *still* ask for more. In fact, I say you *must* ask for more. More of the good stuff. More of life. More of Jesus.

More *for* us instead of *from* us.

More connection, more freedom, more joy, more peace, and more power to obey God's calling on our lives.

But how do we do this, and what does it look like in real life? In the life of laundry and cranky kids or bosses, burnt dinners, sickness and unpaid bills? How do we get to a place where we even want to ask for more from God in a less-is-more world? How do we even know what is affecting our abilities to do that?

> *The fixes we seek in an attempt to settle our souls often do nothing more than shake our spirits. They often don't fix our problem and can even worsen our feelings and add to our stress about the situation.*

First, let's look at the goal. Let's look at where we want to end up after this journey together—to be whole and holy, to stand right before God and live our lives to the fullest potential He has deemed possible for us busy mamas.

So we'll start all the way at the very beginning—with *wholeness*.

## What Does It Mean to Be Whole?

How often do you start something and then don't get to complete it? This happens all the time, which is why there are so many self-help resources for managing our lives. A quick search online will pull up thousands of books, articles, and blogs on how to better manage your time, be a good friend, declutter your home, be a great employee, make better decisions, take your marriage to the next level, and so on.

There is even a book on how to buy a self-help book. True story. What I am saying is there are a lot of fixes for our issues.

Have you tried any of them? Some work great. Last year, I found a cleaning schedule via Pinterest, and it was phenomenal . . . for the first two weeks. Another time, I found a user-friendly system to streamline my finances and set a budget . . . until the system couldn't handle my varied sources of income and expenses.

The fixes we seek in an attempt to settle our souls often do nothing more than shake our spirits. They often don't fix our problem and can even worsen our feelings and add to our stress about the situation.

> *The small pieces of our lives that seem separate from one another actually work together to complete who we are, because we have a Creator who speaks through our pieces from a place of true wholeness.*

So I have a different thought on the idea of "fixing." While there are plenty of tactics to help manage life, can we completely fix our lives or get rid of the stress? I hate to say it, but no.

We live in a crazy, sin-filled world where reality is raw and messy. That, my friends, won't change until the day Jesus comes back.

However, I *do* believe we can learn to embrace the raw and messy and live a whole life now, not trying to find the next fix but navigating the essence of living wholly.

**Because God's Truth is this universe's one true reality. Jesus is our fix.**

Everything else we experience, see, and feel is filtered through the world and all it entails. We look at each segment of our day-to-day—the laundry, the women's brunch, the work conference call, the date night, the carpooling to gymnastics—and think these are different compartments and roles in our lives. While related, they are ultimately separate. This is how our human brains naturally work and are able to focus on more than one thing at a time.

Compartmentalization is a subconscious defense mechanism our minds employ to avoid cognitive anxiety or discomfort.

But the reality is that our lives are not split up into "working professional" or "mom" or "wife" or any other label, but instead are whole and holy authentic together as one. While it's easier on us to separate each perceivably different compartment of our lives so life doesn't feel so disjointed, God doesn't see the separation, nor does He intend for anything about our lives to be compartmentalized. It's all intertwined and directly related to make up who we are meant to be.

> And we know that for those who love God all
> things work together for good, for those who are
> called according to his purpose. (Romans 8:28)

The small pieces of our lives that seem separate from one another actually work together to complete who we are, because we have a Creator who speaks through our pieces from a place of true wholeness.

Recognizing this is the first step in putting back the pieces of our lives into a wholly mended and eventually holy life.

> Now may the God of peace make you holy in
> every way, and may your whole spirit and soul
> and body be kept blameless until our Lord Jesus
> Christ comes again. God will make this happen,
> for he who calls you is faithful.
> (1 Thessalonians 5:23-24 NLT)

Before we move on, I want to mention that in 1 Thessalonians 5:23-24, Paul talks about the whole person—spirit, soul, and body. You cannot have one without the other. Your spirit has a soul that must have a body to live in and through; all three are interwoven.

We know we need to strive to keep our bodies healthy, and there are plenty of books and experts on physical health, so here we're talking more about the health of our spirit and soul and what they crave, more than our physical bodies. Know, though, that they are all intertwined and related.

*Our bodies naturally crave to be whole, and our spirit and soul crave the completeness they lack on their own. They need the intervention of God to bring them back.*

To be whole, each aspect of a person must be well. When one portion is wounded, injured, or impaired, the other portions are affected.

So, let's look at definitions to make sure we don't misunderstand one another in our discussion of what *wholeness* means.

The word *whole* means containing all components, not being divided or wounded, and the whole is a system made up of interrelated parts.

Did you catch that? It contains *all* components and is not divided. When did we learn to divide our thinking rather than look at the complete picture of who we are?

I know I keep referencing food and diets, but it's because they are a great example of what I'm talking about. Plus, I'm always hungry.

When planning a new diet or lifestyle to shape the health of our physical bodies, we can start with the common knowledge that the more whole foods we eat, the better. If you look up the term "whole foods" you'll find they are unprocessed and unrefined plant foods (or processed and refined as little as possible) before being consumed. Basically, they are still in their natural state, the state nature intended for them to be in and the state our bodies naturally crave.

**Our bodies naturally crave to be whole, and our spirit and soul crave the completeness they lack on their own. They need the intervention of God to bring them back.**

I've been known to look to complete myself through all kinds of outside influences. When I was single, I looked for a husband to "complete me" (are you getting flashbacks from *Jerry Maguire* right now?). When I knew I had talents and skills to offer the world, I looked to complete that yearning through hobbies and work. When I was simply bored, I would fill myself with semitrashy television (Any other lovers of *The Bachelor*? Anyone?) or a new DIY project at home (I want to grow up to be Joanna Gaines someday) that would make me feel better about my own love life, work, and home.

*He created us to have space inside that only His Spirit can fill. And He created everything surrounding that space to work toward that space. Even what we do.*

But did they complete me? No.

We can and do look to fill the void areas of our lives with "things" and "fixes" that the world can offer us.

But the void can only be filled by Jesus. It is shaped just like Him because He is our Creator.

The void shape of loving on our slightly obnoxious neighbor, the mold of respecting our harsh boss because we know Jesus would, the shell of grace and compassion when our children screw up. He created us to have space inside that only His Spirit can fill. And He created everything surrounding that space to work *toward* that space. Even what we do.

## *Created to Work*

Psalm 139:14 says we are "fearfully and wonderfully made." In the original Hebrew, "the word 'fearfully' means: with great reverence, heart-felt interest and with respect. The word 'wonderfully' means: unique, set apart, marvelous."[2]

This is how God created both Adam and Eve and how He's made each of us. Adam and Eve were both unique, different from each other, and He made them differently—He created Adam from dust and Eve from Adam's rib. Similarly, He created you differently from me. He made all of us humans unique from all other creation because we were created in His image (Genesis 1:27).

In the beginning, Adam and Eve were whole.

Something to note when reading the Book of Genesis is that Adam and Eve were whole once *together and with* God. In relationship with each other and with Jesus.

I know, it was easy before sin entered our world, right? To be together and with God in harmony. Before we had jobs and babies and grumpy bosses and five o'clock traffic.

While babies weren't in the picture yet for Adam and Eve—because we're still really early on in this relationship with the two lovebirds—the Bible doesn't shy away from the fact that they were set to work already. Genesis 2:15 says God put Adam in the garden of Eden to "work it and keep it." He also made Eve in order to be not only a companion but also a "helper" to Adam (Genesis 2:18-22).

Not only was Adam created to work but Eve was as well.

And so are we. Whether that's at home, in an office, in our church, or wherever.

Our situation is different, though, because we are on the other side of Eve's sin. That same enemy who ninjaed her mind into thinking it was best to disobey God by eating from the tree of the knowledge of good and evil is the same enemy who ninjas his way into our lives. He whispers lies that tug at our thoughts, breaking us down emotionally, physically, and therefore spiritually while we live out this mom life.

These whispered lies chip off and scatter the pieces of our wholeness across work, home, and relationships. They break us and cause us to see the pieces of our lives as separate and not whole.

The sin in our world is what causes the brokenness and the pieces of our whole selves to come apart.

## Picking Up the Pieces

Remember those details of our crazy day-to-day lives we talked about earlier? The loose sheets and varied range of things we deal with every day? They are the hundreds of tiny pieces that make up a whole life—a portfolio life.

Maybe you're still wondering what the pieces look like in your life. Not only do we know them by the crazy they make us feel, but we can recognize them by listening and feeling for the chipping away of our peace.

Pieces fall apart when we hear our coworkers or our boss make rude remarks about motherhood and how it affects work life, and we feel angry. I (often!) drop a piece here and there when on social media I see that other moms take fabulous vacations because they have jobs that allow them to afford these vacations or that other moms are at the park with their little ones *again* because their jobs don't require them to be in an office every day the way mine does. Pieces slip when our spouses forget to acknowledge how hard we worked on getting the house clean on our only day off, for the love. A forgotten piece is hidden in a corner when we rush through our daily and weekly checklists of what to do, where to be, and who to call.

It's hard. Sin causes emotions, thoughts, and even actions of ours to keep us from our completed lives in Christ. So, not surprisingly, after all of this we become timid, defensive, bruised, sometimes even resentful. But I think we're ready. Ready to pick up the pieces of our rushed day-to-day and mend them back into a whole life.

> *He doesn't expect anything more from you or me because* He is *the more. And He isn't waiting for you or me to get it all together because He knows* He is *the all we need to have it together.*

Can I share a secret with you? I don't believe you and I are incomplete and *not* whole. I can't believe it. I believe we are already whole because Christ is in us. This is our truth, as believers and followers of Christ. But we need to live it out.

Is it that we have forgotten—or never been told?—who we are and why we're here? Do we not see all the pieces that make us whole? When I look around, I see things that make my heart hurt and my head angry for the moms of our generation.

I see women who believe life is meant to be always moving.
I see women who believe and live the lie that motherhood is
   the highest calling.
I see women who believe their worth is based on the quality of
   their work.
I see women who believe they are what people tell them they
   are—beautiful, ugly, skinny, fat, hardworking, lazy, simple,
   complex . . .

Again, have we forgotten who we really are and why we're here?

# Mended and Whole

Allow me to remind you, my friend, of who you really are and what makes you whole.

> You are created in the image of God. (Genesis 1:27)
> You are filled with the breath of God. (Genesis 2:7)
> You are not to be shamed. (Genesis 2:25)
> You were created to work and keep God's creations.
>   (Genesis 2:15)
> You are good. (Genesis 1:31)

Not only did God bless you, breathe His holy and pure breath into you, shape you into His likeness, and trust you to take care of His creation, He also called you "good." The same "good" He called the sun that gives us light and the stars that rule the universe; the same "good" He called the majestic mountain peaks when He gathered dry land together, separate from the expansive oceans and seas; the same "good" He called every winged bird and every fruit-bearing tree.

You are good, *just like that.*

Everything that makes up you—the natural, unrefined-by-the-world, *real* you—is good.

The God of completeness doesn't call anything "good" that isn't whole and doesn't reflect Him.

This includes all aspects of your days—the laundry piles you tear down so your family has clean clothes, the sales calls you make to enhance a potential customer's life, the carpooling you navigate to help another mama out, the late-night emails you answer because you have clients waiting, and the dinner you prepare for the family.

These are *all good things* He made you for. Not just one or two of them, or whatever you have time for in any given day or season. He has called you to *all of it*. All of it makes up the whole of your life and the calling on your life.

> *We will become whole by believing God at His Word. We don't need something or someone telling us there are separate sides to this thing we call life, because we have a Reality that offers this work-hard mom life peace, contentment, and joy through the whole of it.*

It's sad, but I forget that God is the main character and I am— we are—the supporting cast. It's not just convenient to remember that; it's necessary.

Because God has got this—completely and wholly. He doesn't expect anything more from you or me because *He is* the more. And He isn't waiting for you or me to get it all together because He knows *He is* the all we need to have it together.

He is the whole enchilada. The One with the biggest influence on our lives, who wraps us up and hems us in, completing us.

When we accept Christ into our lives, we become whole. We are no longer the broken and scattered scraps of Eve's consumed apple. We are finally back to a quality or state of being without restriction, exception, or qualification, just as whole and unprocessed as nature intended.

So, no, it's not time to balance the scale, with mom on one side and everything else on the other. It's time to throw that scale out because there aren't *two* sides to your life. Your life is your *one* life.

We will be content and embrace our day-to-day, our relationships, our work, and the entirety of our reality. We will find peace in our wholeness through our proper perspective with God as the main character in our story. We will become whole by believing God at

His Word. We don't need something or someone telling us there are separate sides to this thing we call life, because we have a Reality that offers this work-hard mom life peace, contentment, and joy through the whole of it.

And it is good.

## Notes

1. "Working Mothers Issue Brief," Women's Bureau: US Department of Labor, June 2016, www.dol.gov/wb/resources/WB_WorkingMothers _508_FinalJune13.pdf.

2. Craig A. Nelson, *The Physiology of Faith: Fearfully and Wonderfully Made to Live and Prosper in Health* (Bloomington, IN: WestBow, 2015), chapter 2.

# Holy Moly

O Lord, who shall sojourn in your tent?
    Who shall dwell on your holy hill?

He who walks blamelessly and does what is
right
    and speaks truth in his heart;
who does not slander with his tongue
    and does no evil to his neighbor,
    nor takes up a reproach against his friend;
in whose eyes a vile person is despised,
    but who honors those who fear the
    Lord;
who swears to his own hurt and does not
change;
who does not put out his money at interest
    and does not take a bribe against the
    innocent.
He who does these things shall never be moved.
                         (Psalm 15)

A few months after I was born, my parents, older brother, and I moved overseas to execute my dad's military orders in Wiesbaden, Germany. After three years of overseas service and after adding my sister to the clan, our family was ordered back home to the States.

The five of us flew out of Rhein-Main Air Base just opposite of the Frankfurt Airport. As most airports do, the air base had gates, but instead of providing a jet bridge for passengers to walk directly onto the plane, it had buses that took passengers from the gate to wherever the airplane waited on the tarmac. I'm not sure how long our particular ride was across the tarmac; we couldn't see the plane from the gate and had to drive around a building or two to get to it.

My family loaded onto the bus first and spread across the first row of seats behind the driver. Mom, with baby Katie in her lap, and my brother sat directly behind the driver, while Dad and I sat in the seat opposite them. I don't remember any of these details, but Dad tells me Stuart and I were excited and wanted to look out the over-sized front windows of the bus as we drove.

As the driver pulled away from the gate, passengers sat in relative silence, bumping along over the tarmac. As we rounded a final corner, our massive 747 jet stood waiting there.

I mean, *right* there. Filling up the entire window in front of us. Before anybody could say anything, my three-year-old pithy self screamed, "*Holy cow!*"

The whole bus heard it and cracked up because—confession—I may have used a different word in place of "cow." A word that isn't quite appropriate for someone writing about Jesus. Thanks for the great example of stellar diction, Mom and Dad.

The huge jet was overwhelming to my little three-year-old mind and body. So, without thinking and in my state of trance and awe, I exclaimed out loud.

My parents, on the other hand, knew what was coming around the corner, so they weren't surprised. On our bus journey, even though they couldn't see it, my parents expected the jet to be as large and awesome as it was. However, when I saw its massiveness, my mind was blown.

Friend, our ride to whole and holy doesn't have to be a surprise. We can be more like my parents on that bus than my three-year-old self. We won't need any expression of surprise because we'll expect what's at our destination.

God's presence is our desired destination, and His presence is holy.

As believers, we've already arrived at the destination of holiness. We have glimpses and expectations, given to us through Scripture, of how magnificent, breathtaking, and glorious His holiness is. Scripture describes the holiness of God by saying,

> Who is like You among the gods, O Lord?
> Who is like You, majestic in holiness,
> Awesome in praises, working wonders?
> (Exodus 15:11 NASB)

and

> "There is no one holy like the Lord,
> Indeed, there is no one besides You,
> Nor is there any rock like our God."
> (1 Samuel 2:2 NASB)

Words such as *wonder, awesome,* and *majestic* are used to describe Him and His holiness. And He is here, available to us, and just waiting for us to recognize it.

## *What Are We Working Toward?*

To be holy isn't the motivation I wake up to every day. It's not the goal I set each day and hope to achieve before nightfall. I don't sit down and say, "Hmm . . . how can I live holy today?"

Nope. It's just not the language or thought process I use, especially before my morning coffee. But something I *do* work toward, and I believe everyone else does, is happiness. Or better yet, joy. I wake up and do the things that will make me joyful or try to get me there. We all want to be joyful and content. This is not a secret.

However, what most of us don't recognize is that contentment and joy are found on the path of holy living. We will never find these things if we don't first look for holiness. Holiness is the only path with contentment and joy stationed along the way.

> *We search and search and set happiness at the end of the path we're stumbling down. But happiness comes along the way. It meets us along the route rather than at the destination.*

While we will probably find things that make us happy along the walk down the path, they are the external things that trigger feelings of pleasure. They're the outside influences on our lives. These are what determine happiness, which is a temporary thing.

Joy, on the other hand, is cultivated internally and is much more consistent, closer to the destination and final resting place of contentment with who, why, and how we are.

Joy and contentment shine bright in our periphery, even on days we are so bogged down with toddlers, teenagers, and tempers from what seems like every person in our lives. We want to be there with them, peaceful and joyful even in our bogged-down days.

> *Ultimately, it boils down to the fact that*
> *God, as our Creator, is the One who brings*
> *us happiness and joy—both external and*
> *internal. And the only way we can get to Him*
> *is through His holy Son, Jesus.*

However, joy and contentment linger just outside the window of busy and distracted. They are out there taunting us, saying if we could just wrap up the current projects or situations and make room for them, they'll come in. We need to finish emptying the dishwasher and cleaning house. We need to get that promotion or make enough money to take that vacation. We need to get our houses and children in a perpetual state of order and tidiness. Once all of this is done, *then* they can join us. *Then* we can be joyful and content.

We chase joy. We rush around finishing things to get us there. It's why there are so many self-help options out there. We do the things—*all* the things—that walk us in that direction. We:

- read books, blogs, and articles on joy and how to be happy.
- schedule time to meet up with friends, busying our already busy calendar.
- research, apply for, and work at jobs that match our skill sets and passions.
- exercise and take care of our bodies.
- get eight hours of sleep each night.

The list goes on.

Hear me when I say these things aren't bad. They are good, and I believe we should do them. But we must recognize that *these are not the things* that will bring us joy. Sure, they can contribute to it and bring about temporary happiness, but they aren't the answer.

I love what Eleanor Roosevelt once said: "Happiness is not a goal, it's a by-product."

We search and search and set happiness at the end of the path we're stumbling down. But happiness comes along the way. It meets us along the route rather than at the destination. It will not just walk alongside, but it will run, skip, stumble, backtrack, and even stop to rest with us on this journey.

However, we still wonder where this happiness is waiting for us. We forget that happiness is determined by external sources, but true *joy*—well, that's found elsewhere. Which path is it waiting for us on? It's not on just any trail of life, but—again—on the path to holy living.

And holiness is attributed to God.

Ultimately, it boils down to the fact that God, as our Creator, is the One who brings us happiness and joy—both external and internal. And the only way we can get to Him is through His holy Son, Jesus. John 14:6 says, "I am the way, and the truth, and the life. No one comes to the Father except through me."

So, we work to get holy and get to God. Got it. We work to be more like Him and understand who He is by

- going to church.
- listening and singing (loudly) to worship music in the car.
- having time alone with God every day before work.
- praying before bed.
- reading the Bible.
- sending our kids to youth group.
- making casseroles for new neighbors or friends who've just had a baby or lost a loved one.
- joining a small group.
- attending Christian conferences.
- memorizing Bible verses.
- volunteering in the church nursery.

Check. Check. Check.

Whew. I'm exhausted even reading through this list. But because I did these things, I'm "holy," right?

Wrong.

> *We must realize that our holiness isn't about anything we do but about what Christ has already done.*

I can do all of these things and *still* not be holy. I can try and work and exhaust myself with these things holy people do and still not come out on the holy side of things.

We strive and do and strive and do some more to be like Christ.

But the thing that proves our Christlikeness more than anything else—more than how often I read my Bible or volunteer at the homeless shelter or make it to church service on time—is our holiness. The nature and character of Christ expressed through us, His *holiness* in us, is what aligns and illuminates Christ more than our skills in sales strategizing or in the kitchen. More than our quiet time habits or church attendance. And, dare I say, even more than our faith in Jesus.

We know this because there are examples of those who have faith that Jesus is in fact the Son of God but who still are not holy.

> You believe that God is one; you do well. Even
> the demons believe—and shudder!
>
> (James 2:19)

To say I'm "holy" sounds like a big, bad statement from someone who is just trying to keep her head above water. Is it just me, or does this seem like a circle going nowhere? I want to be holy, so I do holy things, but those things still don't make me holy. What's the secret? *Is* there a secret formula?

We must realize that our holiness isn't about anything *we* do but about what Christ has *already done.*

He has already paid the price of our sin, to clear our names on Judgment Day. His death and subsequent resurrection removed us from death row. Removed us from alignment with the world and set us apart in a holy place, connected with God.

> *The culture we live in wants us to join in,*
> *not separate ourselves. So anything holy is*
> *offensive to this world we live in.*

If we stand firm in this truth, knowing with our entire being that Jesus is our Savior and He was the *only* sacrifice powerful enough for us to be close to and connected with God, then we are holy.

And that's it. We are *already* holy.

Mind blown.

## A Four-Letter Word

*Holy.*

Our culture has morphed the term *holy* into a common intensive used to strengthen an exclamation. Often, it's even thrown in front of an offensive four-letter word.

It's funny though; *holy* is literally a four-letter word. Our idea of "four-letter words" tends to be those that are coarse, offensive, and frowned upon when used in public settings, not anything that is holy.

But if you think about it, anything holy should be—and is— offensive to this world. The offense is not in the noun, the explicit word, but in the adjective that describes it.

OK, stay with me here, and let's talk about the definition of *holy*, both from a heavenly and a worldly perspective.

The word *holy* actually means to be "worthy of complete devotion."[1]

Have you thought about what slang terms like "holy cow" mean? Or insert whatever jargon you desire. Whatever you choose, it's rather comical. When used like this, it means this cow is worthy of complete devotion. Now, if you're into whole milk and cheese-burgers, then sure; to each his own.

Ask any churchgoing person, and I'll bet he'd tell you that to be holy means to be "set apart." It's something different. Something not like anything else.

However, this isn't how our world works. It doesn't like loners. The culture we live in wants us to join in, not separate ourselves.

So anything holy is offensive to this world we live in.

In our example of "holy cow," it's not *cow*, but the fact that the noun is *holy* that is offensive. The world wants you to focus on *anything* but what is holy—God or the relationships He's given us. This side of heaven is stalked by a real-life enemy, one who wants you so absorbed with thinking and acting like the rest of the world that you will be clueless—or misinformed—about what God's Word says about Him or you.

Our culture wants you to shift your focus and give in to the idea that we must look, act, even work like all the other women, and sometimes even men. It wants us to believe we must choose to focus all our attention on hitting our work deadline or coming up with the perfect, impressive dish for supper club. It wants us to look at the woman in the next cubicle and convince ourselves she has it all together while we're just lucky not to have on a shirt stained with coffee or breast milk or both. It wants us to insert our not-so-compassionate opinion on the latest viral political social media post—and then keep checking back on it to see who has "liked" our comment.

Psalm 9:3 says, "When my enemies turn back, they stumble and perish before your presence." In my English Standard Version, the notes at the bottom say this verse can also be worded "they stumble and perish because of your presence."

Um, OK. That's scary, right? *Because of* God's holiness, anything near Him that is not holy will perish.

The Old Testament explains how the people of Israel erected the Tabernacle a year after Passover. It was the visual dwelling place of God with His people in the wilderness. Basically, it was a tent. But this tent wasn't like the ones we pitch ourselves in the "wilderness" of a state park with RV hookups for water and electricity. This was where God hung out with His people.

OK, that's not completely accurate. God didn't really chill with His people and watch Netflix or laugh over a glass of pinot at the kitchen table. He stationed Himself inside what was called the *most holy place* or the *Holy of Holies*, a sectioned-off portion inside the tent. A thick curtain separated this spot from the rest of the tent.

I picture my fourth-grade daughter, stationing herself on the recliner, away from the rest of us squished together on another couch with Netflix. She's got her own spot and nobody—especially little sisters—had better enter her personal space or, *woo-wee*, the wrath will reign.

(OK, so the recliner and my daughter's "personal space" are nowhere near synonymous with the Holy of Holies and God's own righteousness, but sometimes the female hormones and sibling rivalries sure can make it *feel* like a heavy curtain has fallen through the living room. I know all my fellow moms of hormonal girls can relate.)

Nobody could enter this separated place because it shielded a holy God from sinful man. Only the high priest could enter on one day a year—the Day of Atonement.

Can we talk for a minute about how exhausting the process to be near God must have been for the high priest? The high priest was required to wash himself, put on a special outfit, and bring burning incense to prevent his eyes from seeing God directly, as well as blood to make atonement for sins. Anyone or anything that entered this spot was entering the *very literal presence* of God, so preparations were a must.

Side note. I know a few men today who wouldn't have survived this process without a woman's detailed help and guidance. While I am in awe of that high priest, I am also convinced that his mama was probably involved in the process. Having to make the major preparations required *surely* would have led to a missed detail somewhere had he done it himself. Most men I know just don't have the attention to detail a woman does. That's why I believe his mama headed up this Get-Ready-for-God operation.

Anyway, back to the point. The curtain separating God from the rest of the tent was crucial because anything near God that wasn't holy would burn up or evaporate or succumb to some other sort of immediate death. God cannot, by His nature, tolerate sin, and His eyes are too pure to look at evil (Habakkuk 1:13), so the veil made sure people couldn't carelessly stumble into His awesome presence and melt away like the Wicked Witch of the West.

> When everything had been arranged like this,
> the priests entered regularly into the outer room
> to carry on their ministry. But only the high
> priest entered the inner room, and that only
> once a year, and never without blood, which he

offered for himself and for the sins the people
had committed in ignorance.

(Hebrews 9:6-7 NIV)

So, here's what we know so far:

- Anything holy is worthy of our complete devotion.
- Anything holy cannot be of or near this world.
- Whatever is *not* holy cannot be near God.

We've looked at the definition of *holy*, but let's look elsewhere, as well. When we link the word *holy* to the God of the universe and how He defines it through the Bible, we dig up more on how it relates to us and our lives.

As we established, the Greek word for "holy" or "sacred" is *hagios*. It means "set apart." Check. We got that definition. Set apart by or for God.

I'm such a word nerd, looking up stuff like this makes me seriously giddy. So you can imagine the stupid grin and wide eyes on my face when I looked up the word online and read that anything *hagios* is "properly reverend, worthy of veneration." Anything that is *holy* is something possessing a certain sacred distinction and is not to be profaned.

Which is us, right? *Right?*

Well, according to the Bible, it is. Or at least it should be. It tells us in Leviticus 11, 19, 20, 21 and Deuteronomy 23 *and* 1 Peter 2 that because God is holy, we—and the things we do, eat, wear, and so on—should be holy.

OK, yeah, yeah . . . we know we are to be holy, because God is holy.

But wow . . . me? Us? *Holy?*

It sure doesn't feel like it.

I guarantee it's not holy to scream at my kids to pick up their clothes for the seventy billionth time in ten minutes or to intentionally delete an email from a slightly obnoxious coworker or to roll over in bed hoping my husband will think I'm asleep.

I am a sinner. We are all sinners. We screw up every day. We think terrible thoughts when a coworker saunters in wearing a less-than-appropriate outfit to the board meeting, we raise our voices at our kids about eating their vegetables, we give in to our craving for just one more glass of wine when we know we've had too much, as well as other sinful cravings we know aren't best for us or our relationships.

How can we be holy with all of this swirling through our everyday?

Friend, I admit I am not a rocket scientist, a deep-thinking theologian, or a PhD in *anything*, but I know the answer to this question.

Jesus.

And oh my gosh, it seems that every good little Christian answer is "Jesus."

That's because Jesus is not just *an* answer; He is *the* answer.

> *Our world needs more holy people. More believers in God's Son. More people who maybe aren't perfect but represent His perfection. Who aren't purehearted but exemplify His pure heart in the limelight.*

Remember how I mentioned the high priest was the only one who could enter the holiest of holy places in the Tabernacle? He had a huge checklist of stuff to do before he could enter God's presence to make himself holy enough to *not die*. He cleaned himself and brought blood for atonement for sins. And not just his sins, but the sins of the poor people waiting anxiously outside the Tabernacle to be saved as well.

Jesus, when He went to the cross, was cleaned and purified already. He then offered *His* blood for our sins. That afternoon on the cross was powerful enough to carry across land and oceans to atone for the sins of people—*all* people—and not just those waiting and watching anxiously there in front of Him at the foot of the cross. It carried not only geographically but also over time through generations past, present, and future.

> *Holiness is what gives us credibility to share about Christ with our kids, coworkers, and friends.*

That's us, friend. It carried over to *us*.
So now, when God looks at us, He sees Jesus.
He sees a clean and pure child of His.

> But when Christ came as high priest of the good things that are now already here, he went through the greater and more perfect tabernacle that is not made with human hands, that is to say, is not a part of this creation. He did not enter by means of the blood of goats and calves; but he entered the Most Holy Place once for all by his own blood, thus obtaining eternal redemption. (Hebrews 9:11-12 NIV)

Did your heart just leap with a rush of adrenaline at that thought? Mine did. What a crazy image.

When I look at myself in the mirror, I see . . . well, myself.

I see gray hairs glistening through the grown-out hair dye, wrinkles carving into the skin around my eyes, and post-baby weight that shifted and brought heavier friends to more unfortunate areas of my body. I see someone who worries about what people think of her house and what her kids are wearing, someone who wonders if what she said in the department meeting sounded smart enough.

When *God* looks at me, He sees perfection, a pure heart, a sinless and holy person.

Our world needs more holy people. More believers in God's Son. More people who maybe aren't perfect but represent His perfection. Who aren't purehearted but exemplify His pure heart in the limelight.

Our culture tends to value gifts, talents, and resources in ourselves and others, but do we value holiness? Do we value the people and not just what they do, but who they are? Do we value the price paid in blood on that cross some two thousand years ago?

We may say we do, but do we? Do we really?

Holiness is what gives us credibility to share about Christ with our kids, coworkers, and friends. If we tell others how our lives have changed but don't live a changed life or one that looks different from everyone else's life, we won't be effective in witnessing to the power of Christ in our lives.

Hear me again when I say we don't have to intentionally do anything to be holy. Christ made all His believers holy by His work on the cross. Our belief in the sacrifice He made for us is enough to propel us to walk out a life that is different from the one the world walks.

We discussed in the first chapter how foods in their most natural state are considered whole, and in our natural state, we were created to be whole. The same is true for holiness.

God called us good when we were created. He does not—*cannot*—say something is good if it is not whole, reflecting Him in creation. So just as we are complete and whole in Christ in our creation, then we are also holy in our faith in Him.

We say it's our humanness or natural state to [enter whatever sinful behavior you wish], but actually, if we were created in holiness and wholeness, our sinful behavior is not merely to be human but to be "qualitatively subhuman," to be separated from God.[2]

So, in order to be completely human and be near God, we must become Christlike and holy.

It's worth noting holiness affects our health. J. I. Packer wrote, "Holiness is actually the true health of the person. Anything else is ugliness and deformity at character level; a malfunctioning of the individual; a crippled state of soul."[3]

The New Testament shares how Jesus healed people physically. It's interesting that when He did this, He healed not only their physical state but their inner state as well. He put people back on a path of spiritual growth and health. It was not uncommon for writers in the New Testament to begin or end their letters with greetings and wishes for good health, both physical and spiritual. It's a truth known today as well: complete health includes both physical and spiritual components.

Remember when we took our babies and toddlers every few months to their well-child checkups at the pediatrician's office? The doctor charted how much our kiddos grew between visits because there was a standard for healthy growth. If our child wasn't growing as he or she should, then it would alert us that something was wrong. So we might offer better-quality foods, perhaps more physical activity, and balance that with rest and play.

As parents, we are expected to offer the necessary tools for our children to grow—healthy food, protection, and ways to physically move about. In the same way, God offers us everything we need to grow physically and spiritually. We know this because Matthew 6 tells us that He already knows what we need and that we will receive it.

> Do not be like them, for your Father knows
> what you need before you ask him. . . . For the
> pagans run after all these things, and your heav-
> enly Father knows that you need them.
> (Matthew 6:8, 32 NIV)

*Holiness on this side of heaven is a work in progress.*

We are human and we are sinners—spiritually sick, so to speak—so our sanctification and literal holiness will not be fully complete until we are in heaven. However, we are commanded as believers to seek His holiness, and through our faith His holiness is imparted to us.

So in order to keep our belief firm and rooted in Christ and to seek holiness as we are commanded to, we must continue to offer ourselves spiritual food to nourish our faith, opportunities to physically move our faith (through prayer and reading God's Word), and rest to provide balance .

Being spiritually healthy is a necessity.

So where do we start? With a new agreement about what it means to "be holy" on this side of heaven.

## *A New Agreement*

It's funny, I don't know anything about what it means to be inherently holy. But here I am, writing about holiness. Our world pressures us to conform, not to set ourselves apart, and many times we succumb to living blended in the world.

We may not know anything about being holy, but God knows everything about it.

> *We can only see a step, maybe two, ahead of us. But Jesus, at the other end, sees a brightly lit, righteous and holy path that radiates everything His name represents— love, joy, peace, patience, kindness, goodness, faithfulness, and self-control.*

And in the end, that's what matters. Because He's taking care of it for us. He's the one who set us apart. He set a place for us in heaven, and He's set our daily path in front of us, a path that is different and set apart from this world's path.

Now, we have to agree to stand and walk on that holy ground, understanding that when God looks at us, He sees Jesus.

That's our part. Our only requirement in this life is to agree that God has given us a new direction to walk that is different from the direction of our nonbelieving friends traveling next to us.

Want to know a secret truth about holiness?

A holy life is not a perfect life. It is merely a life set apart.

Can I get all the praise-hand emojis for the fact we do not have to be perfect? Because *pressure*. I've got enough issues I'm tackling day to day without having to think about being perfect at all the things. And I know you do too.

We don't have to feel holy all the time or be perfect, because Jesus already did that for us.

Psalm 23:2-3 says, "He leads me beside still waters. He restores my soul. He leads me in paths of righteousness for his name's sake."

This path? It looks dark from our vantage point. We can only see a step, maybe two, ahead of us. But Jesus, at the other end, sees a brightly lit, righteous and holy path that radiates everything His name represents—love, joy, peace, patience, kindness, goodness, faithfulness, and self-control.

(Did you sing those fruits of the Spirit along with me? Thank you, VBS, for forever adding harmonies and rhythm to this fruit.)

I imagine this path winding next to a stream, one that isn't rushing and bubbling. One that is still and unchanging. One that is deep and wide. It's not like the rushing flow of streams and rivers we have on this side of heaven. It's quiet and allows us to rest and drink from it in between the crazy. It restores our souls to a place of contentment and rest even while we're surrounded by the hustle and bustle of school drop-offs, overflowing email in-boxes, PTA meetings, football practices and games, laundry without end, board meetings, take-out lunch, dinner, and all the other things.

It's time we let God have the gratitude deserved of Him and take back our mind-sets that this crazy life has stolen. According to Psalm 24:1, God has claimed the world and everything in it. Let's stop letting the world claim us, and remember who we belong to.

This sounds great, right? But what now?

How do we find the path, the stream of still waters—and stay there—in the middle of the chaos that is life?

We can agree we are whole and holy in Christ, but how do we live a life set apart when all we want to do is live a life that simply doesn't kill us in the process of motherhood?

This thing we're doing? This mom thing, this wife thing, this single thing, this work thing, this Jesus thing, this *life* thing?

It's hard.

I know this and you know this. But maybe we begin to understand that even in the hard, even in the big picture and the little picture, we can and are already living complete and holy and good through and because of Jesus.

And may we stand in awe of the sheer magnitude of His crazy love for us that towers over and around us. May we shout holy words that praise His righteousness and our salvation.

41

And may we agree, believe, and stand in agreement that we live a life set apart from others and that when God sees us, He sees Jesus.

That's the path we will walk together throughout the rest of this book. We're going to look at each day, each moment, and discover what happens when we believe God has more for us than what we think the sum of our day-to-day equals. God puts breath into us, and we allow Him to be what gets us through each day. We're going to look for and recognize this breath of life that we breathe in and out every day as we mother our children. We're going to see what happens when we believe Him for more in this life.

# *Notes*

1. Merriam-Webster online, s.v. "holy," www.merriam-webster.com /dictionary/holy.

2. See J. I. Packer, *Rediscovering Holiness: Know the Fullness of Life with God* (Colorado Springs: Gospel Light, 2009), 26.

3. Packer, *Rediscovering Holiness*, 34.

# Living This Mom Life

PART 2

CHAPTER 3

# Playing Games

## Keep Away from the Mental Game

As I write this, it is Mother's Day. (Happy Mother's Day, Mama!) I sit here with a blank Word document open on my back patio, trying to get some peace and quiet to write.

This is pretty close to how I've always pictured a book being written; if it wasn't inside a quiet, cozy coffee shop, it was outside with the sun shining, the wind blowing, and the birds chirping.

Granted, it isn't payday yet, so I'm not at Starbucks or the local coffee shop here in town, Cappuccino's. I'm in the shade, not the sun, because of the ninety-plus-degree, muggy, and still Tennessee air. Also, the birds chirping in my backyard are not of the songbird variety, but instead a flock of messy and dirty chickens I made the mistake of agreeing to purchase a couple months ago. Bonus: The dog is whimpering next to me because she wants to eat the chickens, but whatever.

So here I sit, my kids with their cousins down the street and my husband lying on the couch inside nursing his broken bones from a recent bicycle accident.

Want to know my exact thought as I opened my computer and skimmed over my outline for this book?

*I can't do this. There is no way I can write an entire book.*

I don't have the time or the mental capacity to think coherent thoughts, let alone write them down. Everyone in this family is depending on me. Not to mention, I am taking vacation time from my job to handle everything going on at home. My deadline to turn in this manuscript is soon; my kids have huge end-of-the-year school projects and programs (I would like to quit third grade. DONE. I am so over it this year.); I need to register my kids for camps and kindergarten; and we have family coming to town at the end of the month and multiple birthdays to celebrate. To top it off, last week my husband was injured in an accident and forced out of work and onto the couch with me as his nurse for a couple of months. Fun fact: I am not a nurse by trade. Nor am I naturally compassionate toward anyone in my family who may be sick or injured. "Walk it off" is my motto. So my dear husband's extra need for assistance right now is beyond stressful for me during this already busy month.

It's May mayhem around here.

What do I have to say that will help someone else? Who even wants to read words from someone struggling to keep her head above water and not lock herself in a dark closet or purchase a one-way ticket to a deserted island?

Satan is scheming hard to get his way with me right now. Maybe he is antagonizing you too. He has sent his little minions to whisper in our ears that we're not good enough, smart enough, organized enough, creative enough, or caring enough to get our stuff done and handled as it should be. If he's not currently whispering to you, I am willing to bet quite a few dollars that he has told you this in the past and will again sooner rather than later. We all succumb to mental games sometimes.

Some people say, "God just told me . . ." whenever they get a revelation they believe is directly from God.

> *Our thoughts, decisions, and overall mind-*
> *set must live in a holy place, a place set apart*
> *from what our world says is natural for us.*
> *Once our minds are right, our spirits will lead*
> *and then our bodies will follow.*

Now, I've never heard God speak audibly, but thoughts have popped into my brain at times that I think could only be from Him. Like the one thrown into my head as I typed (read: whined to myself) about not being able to write. He said to me:

> *This is what I'm talking about. This is what I need you and others to know. If you think you can't, you won't. If you think **I can**, we **both** will. Stop playing this mind game. Or change the rules in your favor.*

My deeply theological interpretation of this message is that God told me to tell Satan, "COME AT ME, BRO!" And He's telling you the same.

> Submit yourselves therefore to God. Resist the devil, and he will flee from you. Draw near to God, and he will draw near to you. (James 4:7-8)

Yes, we are far from the perfect employees, Christians, friends, wives, or moms we imagined we might be, could be, or want to be, but the devil can bring it on. He won't defeat us, because you and I serve a good and almighty God. His grace is sufficient for us. And when we are weak in mind, He is strong in everything.

## A Self-Fulfilling Prophecy

When God "spoke" this message to me, He also confirmed a modern-day sociological theory we need to remember in order to change the rules and eventually stop playing altogether the mental games we face.

Most of us know the theory of a self-fulfilling prophecy. Our expectation of the prophecy can shape our behavior, causing the prophecy to become reality.

Our thoughts direct our actions. If we don't think something, there is no way our bodies can physically follow. And vice versa. Only when we think something will our bodies follow those thoughts.

Becoming a whole person requires not just setting aside the time mentally to focus—which we'll talk about in chapter 8—but also physically walking down a new cognitive path in a direction where our thoughts end up more biblically inspired. This is where we make the decision that a whole and holy life is what we want. If it is what we want, then we must step out in faith, starting with daily thoughts and decisions.

Our thoughts, decisions, and overall mind-set must live in a holy place, a place set apart from what our world says is natural for us. Once our minds are right, our spirits will lead and then our bodies—actions, words, feelings—will follow.

We need to do this intentionally. We must retrain our minds and redirect them toward a more holy way of processing.

So it's time to work out.

## Building Muscle Memory

I have worked in the cheerleading industry since 2001. When I was still young and able—before birthing multiple children—I worked as an instructor at summer cheerleading camps, and then later moved into a full-time career managing those camps and training a staff of twentysomethings how to teach at them.

The discussion of working out our minds makes me think of something summer-camp instructors are trained to do with campers.

When teaching cheerleaders the correct position for their arms, legs, or core body for a stunt or a motion, it is best to not actually touch the cheerleader, not actually put her body in position *for* her.

> *Scripture needs to be our "camp instructor," carefully directing our thoughts to be whole and holy, not necessarily actively forcing us into a constantly righteous mind-set.*

Instead, instructors are trained to stand in front of the camper to demonstrate with their own correct motion and guide with words ("arms lower," "lunge deeper") until campers are correct. By letting the campers move their own arms to the correct spot, instructors help them create a muscle memory of how to get to that correct place. The cheerleaders can actually feel the change from incorrect to the correct position. They learn to feel when they're wrong, so they can autocorrect and get it—eventually—on their own the first time and without correction.

This isn't much different from what we need to do with our minds. We slowly move our thoughts until they hit the mark. And when they do, we usually know. It feels right.

But we must be careful. What feels "right" to us now, before proper training, may not actually be correct.

It might feel right just because it's the way we've always done it. Like a cheerleader who has always hit her high V motion not in a perfect V shape but with her arms either too close to her head and or too far apart or both, we will never know it's *not* correct positioning without someone to correct us.

So how do we know where our natural tendencies land regarding our thoughts? We self-evaluate and line up the manner of our thinking next to Scripture. We use outside sources to correct our thoughts. We use Scripture as our instructor.

> All Scripture is breathed out by God and profit-
> able for teaching, for reproof, for correction, and
> for training in *righteousness*, that the man of God
> *may be complete*, equipped for every good work.
> (2 Timothy 3:16-17, emphasis mine)

You may have read the first half of this passage many times, but did you catch that last half?

Scripture is to be used so that the man of God may be *complete*. Whole. Breathed out by God for training in *righteousness*. Holy.

Scripture needs to be our "camp instructor," carefully directing our thoughts to be whole and holy, not necessarily actively forcing us into a constantly righteous mind-set.

By allowing us to create muscle memory in our minds of what is correct, not just what "feels" right initially, the Scriptures instruct and train us (2 Timothy 3:16) so that we are equipped and complete (2 Timothy 3:17) for the lives we're living.

Could God just make or force us to always keep our thoughts and mind-set in a holy place, without use of the Scriptures to train and teach? Sure. He's God. He can do whatever He wants.

But He knows us too well.

How often when forced to do something, do we really learn, understand, and soak in the details of that thing? I know I sure don't. I simply go through the motions of what should be done, without a deep understanding.

If God had us always thinking godly thoughts by force, we would lose the reverence and appreciation for the holiness and righteousness of God and His Word. It would become our daily normal.

And yes, holiness as our daily normal is the goal. However, we all have a tendency to take things for granted. We just do. It's human nature to take our "normal" for granted. If we were *forced* into a consistently holy frame of mind, here in this life, we would fail to properly appreciate and lose the necessary reverence for His righteousness and way of thinking due to overfamiliarity.

So we need to train and learn, to create muscle memory for our minds. We start with our current reality and ask questions about it.

What are some of the ways we've always thought about (and therefore reacted to) certain scenarios in our everyday? Think about your day and your reactions to the things thrown at you that send your mind tumbling.

I can come up with a few examples that we may encounter. It's the angry voice mail or text we send when our friend or coworker doesn't return our calls. It's our snarky or resentful response after overhearing someone mention that moms should stay home with their children and not be in the workplace. It's our jealousy when we see friends taking fabulous beach or mountain vacations while we're stuck in the daily grind.

These examples may not be exactly how you'd respond to similar scenarios, but you're human, just like I am, and I'm willing to bet you've had a few thoughts that may be similar.

*If we are going to embrace this whole and holy life, we need to start working our minds out, intentionally bringing our thoughts, and therefore decisions and actions, into a more correct place.*

Anger, resentment, and jealousy are just a few emotions I regularly am forced to balance with my daily commitment to leading a holy life. What are yours?

Whatever your answer is, look into Scripture and line it up next to your life, beginning with Galatians 5.

> Now the works of the flesh are evident: sexual immorality, impurity, sensuality, idolatry, sorcery, enmity, strife, jealousy, fits of anger, rivalries, dissensions, divisions, envy, drunkenness, orgies, and things like these. (Galatians 5:19-21)

Let's ask which of these we experience. We don't have to talk in general either. What about today? I've definitely had or experienced some of the things listed in this verse. Thinking about just today, I can check off:

- strife
- jealousy
- envy
- idolatry
- fit of anger (and Lord, have mercy, was it a fit! About shoes left on the floor, nonetheless. Bless it.)

I won't ask you which "works of the flesh," if any, you deal with, but you may want to ask yourself. The ones I listed are the easiest for me to fall victim to on a daily basis.

Go ahead, list a few. If you don't see the ones you experienced today, think about "things like these," as it says in the verse above.

The problem is these responses feel very normal and sometimes—most times—even justified. Or we wouldn't have felt them, right?

But if we are going to embrace this whole and holy life, we need to start working our minds out, intentionally bringing our thoughts, and therefore decisions and actions, into a more correct place.

We need to have a holy "right" feeling.

We need our brains to create muscle memory of what whole and holy thoughts feel like.

If we read on in Galatians 5, we'll find examples of whole and holy thoughts, feelings, actions, and ways of being. These examples are what the Bible calls fruit of the Spirit.

> But the fruit of the Spirit is love, joy, peace, patience, kindness, goodness, faithfulness, gentleness, self-control; against such things there is no law. (Galatians 5:22-23)

So when you feel any of the above, you know it's a holy feeling.

It's a feeling of humbleness and gentleness.
It's a feeling of joy and peace, patience and love.
It's a feeling of control over our thoughts.
It's the feeling of Galatians 5:22-23.

When we have these feelings, we know we are correctly aligned with God's will for us. In fact, each of these equals one whole singular fruit that is in contrast with the plural works of the flesh—exactly like our one, whole life in Christ contrasts with the compartmentalized view we hold without Christ.

We also don't need to worry if living with these feelings or actions will lead us into sin, separating us from God. That's what Paul means when he says in Galatians 5:23 that "against such things there is no law."

In fact, the opposite will happen. We won't be led into sin;

instead, the Holy Spirit will grow these qualities in our character, allowing us to reflect His holiness. Over time, our muscle memory automatically puts us in a place where we reflect His character instead of our own.

When we're missing one of these fruits of the Spirit, we have a hole. We are filled with holes, like Swiss cheese, instead of being a solid block or slice if we aren't intentionally filling those empty spaces. These holes are the result of our own resentment, jealousy, even comparison to others. We need to evaluate where we're lacking in the fruit of the Spirit and grab hold of those qualities, claiming them as ours. If there's a hole where kindness should be, grab it and work on being kinder, especially when you don't feel like it. If there's a hole where patience should be, intentionally strive to add more patience into your day.

Yes, we will fail sometimes. But I know we can get to a place where we are consistently in a more whole and holy mental state, giving us more joy and peace. We just need to actually work out.

As always, this is the hardest part.

## Workout Plan

I know what you may be thinking: *Kristin, how can I intentionally retrain my brain? I don't even know half the time that there's a more Holy Spirited way to respond until it's too late and I've already responded another way.*

This happens to me all the time. The other day, all three of my kids were taking their sweet time while I tried to rush everyone out the door. After what felt like seven hundred repetitive "Put on your shoes . . . Put on your shoes," I lost it.

I mean, *really* lost it. I screeched as loud as I could that I was leaving without everyone and as soon as I got home, I was throwing away all the shoes in the house—*and* every last toy, just for good measure.

I've never denied falling on the dramatic end of the spectrum.

It wasn't until later that I even considered my response. I just went with my emotions and therefore acted. Without thinking.

I was being reactionary versus purposeful. Looking back, I wish I would have applied both patience and self-control. At the very least, self-control. But patience and self-control didn't even cross my mind until later. All I paid attention to in the moment was that nobody was paying attention to my directions. And I reacted.

So sister, I feel you.

> *We need to think of our thoughts being the ball bounced back and forth between humanness and holiness. We need to keep the ball away from Satan and keep passing it back to the Holy Spirit.*

It's hard. It's hard to stay ahead of our thoughts and actions because a lot of times it's hard to recognize when the negative ones are actually happening.

Something hit me from what I said when I started this chapter. Jesus put this thought in my mind, *Stop playing this mind game. Or change the rules in your favor.*

This mind game. It's a *game.*

A game Satan initiated without my consent and is playing with me without my cooperation. Not cool. He does the same to you too. It's why Ephesians 6 tells us to put on armor against the devil's schemes.

> Take the helmet of salvation, and the sword of the
> Spirit, which is the word of God. (Ephesians 6:17)

Christ is our salvation and has sealed our minds with our salvation and handed us His sword—the Word of God.

We have our weapons ready. So it's time to *knowingly* enter the game and change the rules in our favor.

Remember the childhood game of keep-away in which two or more players pass an item—usually a ball—back and forth, and another player tries to intercept it?

We need to think of our thoughts being the ball bounced back and forth between humanness and holiness. We need to keep the ball away from Satan and keep passing it back to the Holy Spirit. We must take hold of those thoughts and, with the Holy Spirit, keep them in our possession, in a safe place where Satan's schemes can't affect them.

However, in order to know we're even in the game, we need to recognize triggers and then mediate with a few simple—not easy—strategies.

## First, Identify Triggers

This is how you'll know your mental state is heading down a path. In keep-away, if you're the player in the middle, the most effective way to intercept the ball is to look for cues on where the current ball handler will throw it. Does he step to the right or left? Is she about to throw the ball from the chest—a direct line shot—or above her head for a more arched toss?

What triggers your negative mind-sets when they come? What pulls them from a holy place and puts them in a place alongside the world? Which direction are they facing?

If you get defensive after reading emails that lack a kind tone of voice, try picking up the phone in the future and calling people instead of emailing. Online communication has a way of losing a good amount of crucial nonverbal communication cues. Maybe certain email nonverbal tones are your trigger.

If you scroll through social media feeds and tend to find yourself becoming envious, remove the app from your phone so there are fewer tendencies to scroll. With less mindless scrolling, there's less opportunity to feel bouts of jealousy. Maybe feeling upset after scrolling social media is a trigger for you.

If negative people cause you to think negatively, surround yourself with positive people instead. We are products of our environment, and positivity begets positivity. Maybe negative talk is your trigger.

If your family's shoes on the floor is your neat-freak trigger, leading to anger, medicate yourself. (Kidding!)

Maybe instead try offering opportunities for your family to succeed at putting their shoes away by strategically placing shoe collection baskets where the shoes tend to spread out or—better yet—use every stray shoe as a reminder to say a prayer of gratitude for those shoes and the feet that wear them daily. Maybe disorder is your trigger.

In my case, with my slow-moving children, I know I get angry when my kids are still not listening to what I say after fifty repetitions, so I'm going to write down that one of my triggers is hearing myself repeat the same thing over and over. I can then apply Ephesians 6:4 to this scenario and pray the verse in order not to exasperate or anger my kids. My favorite version of this verse is from *The Message*, which says, "Don't exasperate your children by coming down hard on them. Take them by the hand and lead them in the way of the Master."

You know yourself. Take a few minutes to jot down some things that trigger your Galatians 5:19-21 tendencies. Then start paying attention when those things happen so you can be ready to intercede and take charge of your mental game. Writing down the events and situations will help us recognize the triggers and know negative reactions are coming soon.

## Second, Meditate on What Is Good

> Set your minds on things that are above, not on
> things that are on earth. (Colossians 3:2)

Colossians 3:2 is often quoted. I see it on Pinterest all the time. A women's retreat I once attended even spent an entire weekend on it. However, do you know the verses that surround this one? Verse 1 says, "If then you have been raised with Christ, seek the things that are above, where Christ is, seated at the right hand of God."

This is what we're after, right? We're looking for Christ and godly things in our lives to confirm that we are actually whole and holy because we have been raised with Christ.

Right after Colossians 3:2 are verses 3 and 4, saying, "For you have died, and your life is hidden with Christ in God. When Christ who is your life appears, then you also will appear with him in glory."

Here is our confirmation: "Your life is hidden *with* Christ . . . who *is* your life. . . . You also will appear *with him* in glory."

Our life is *with* Christ right now. Remember how we discussed in the last chapter that, because of God's holiness, *anything* near Him that is not holy will perish? We cannot be near or with Him if we are not holy by the blood of Christ.

So what do we do, as holy and complete beings with Christ?

We do Colossians 3:2. We set our minds on things above, heavenly and holy. Our minds must live in a holy place. This is where we think about things that are true, noble, good, and worthy of praise.

> Finally, brothers, whatever is true, whatever is
> honorable, whatever is just, whatever is pure,
> whatever is lovely, whatever is commendable, if
> there is any excellence, if there is anything wor-
> thy of praise, think about these things.
>
> (Philippians 4:8)

Paul is not teaching us the power of positive thinking here. It's important to remember he's teaching us to focus on Scripture-based truth. We can assume this because Scripture is *the* source for knowing these characteristics—truth, honor, righteousness, purity, and so on. We need to set our minds on Scripture-based truths. How do we do this? By reading His Truth. We read our Bibles, memorize verses, and study to understand the core message of what He shares in His Word. When we do this, we gain knowledge to keep in our arsenal, readily available, just as Ephesians 6:17 told us to do. We stand ready to use the "sword of the Spirit" against the enemy.

## Third, Give the Benefit of the Doubt

After the second step, this is the turning point in our mental game. Welcome to the seventh-inning stretch. We're getting up, stretching our "mental legs," and doing something about the remainder of the game.

I've been told that I'm the glass-half-full friend, that I always believe intentions are honest and good, despite contrary evidence, and I offer positive points of view to more negative situations. To say I *always* play up the positive may be a stretch, but for the most part, I try to do this.

It's more simple than it seems. It's not always easy, but it's definitely simple. I choose to believe the best about people. I choose to believe that while these people or situations seem to be threatening our happiness and causing our mental game to slip, they aren't knowingly working to do so.

I believe most people are not trying to upset us, make us jealous, or cause negative reactions in us with their actions or words. And I believe we should all try to think this way.

Now, am I always correct about people in thinking positively? Not by a long shot. People disappoint and have even taken advantage of me. Unfortunately, there are the few exceptions who enjoy causing strife and hurting people.

However, I know that I sincerely desire to please others and God, and I choose to act on the right thing in what I say and do.

So I am going to believe that about others, and I hope you'll learn to, as well. Maybe you already do, even better than I do! Great! By giving the benefit of the doubt, we honor God's people and ultimately Him.

After we give them the benefit of the doubt, it's time to act on our thoughts and holy feelings. It's time to be kind.

## Fourth, Kill Them with Kindness

Make this your life motto: kill them with kindness.

The saying "I could have killed them" has become a pretty standardized way of saying we're angry. If you're in a scenario where you could easily say this, say instead, "I'll kill them . . . with kindness."

Then do it.

If someone or something upsets you, remember these quick points we've already covered:

- You're a player in a mind game.
- You have goodness ready because you set your mind on it constantly.
- You're giving others the benefit of the doubt.

With the fruit of the Spirit, God has graciously given us the ability to choose kindness. He has equipped us for every good work. We know this is true because Hebrews 13:21 says God will "equip you with everything good that you may do his will, working in us that which is pleasing in his sight, through Jesus Christ."

Show kindness and love generously, even—no, *especially*—when you naturally don't want to do so.

When your coworker remarks that he probably would have gone about executing a project in a different way, remember that he has never experienced the trials that your unique job position entails in this exact time and thank him for the input. Maybe even tell him you'll consider his nugget of wisdom for the next project.

When your husband or kids allow your birthday or Mother's Day to go past without so much as an acknowledgment, remember that just as you're thinking of your day (albeit a special one), they are also thinking of *their* day. Maybe offer them a hug and be genuine when you say you're so glad you get to be their wife/mother. Then spend your day with *them*.

When your pregnant friend mentions how she never wants to have any more kids while you're silently begging God for more—or even just one—remember that she's probably worried and scared about having the added responsibility of another child. Affirm her fears and feelings, ask how you can help, and then maybe offer gentle reminders of the blessings children bring to life.

I'm preaching to my sarcastic self here, but be genuine. It may hurt, it may be hard, and you'll probably not want to, but this is the home-run portion of our game, the winning shot at the buzzer.

This four-step process is your brain's muscle memory taking you from what may feel right to a place that is truly correct.

It's our self-fulfilling prophecy, if you will. The way we think leads us to action. Planning the game ahead of time determines the plays we execute. It's where we declare victory.

> But thanks be to God! He gives us the victory
> through our Lord Jesus Christ.
> (1 Corinthians 15:57 NIV)

Meditating on what is good, and setting our minds on heavenly things is the work of Jesus.

Remember what God told me at the beginning of this chapter when I was whining about being overwhelmed?

*If you think you can't, you won't. If you think I can, we both will.*

This is such an important truth for all of us.

Now that we're training for our minds and concentrating on things above and actively taking steps to be kind and give the benefit of the doubt, let's go back to the fruit of the Spirit.

We know all good things come from Him above and all things with God are possible. We know He can do anything.

> Jesus looked at them and said, "With man it is
> impossible, but not with God. For all things are
> possible with God." (Mark 10:27)

And if we do as Paul encouraged the Galatians to do in Galatians 5:25, to "keep in step with the Spirit" (of God), God will do great thing through us. With God's help, we will do it.

> We *both* will make it happen.
> We *both* will play according to His rules, that work in *our* favor.

We *both* will overcome the mental game this world tries to
play.

And eventually, we'll be able to keep away from this game
completely and have peace of mind because we will default to holy
thoughts out of habit.

Game over.

# CHAPTER 4

# Holier Than Thou

## Our Perspective in the Circle of Life

A few years ago, a good friend went into the hospital. Thankfully the issue was minor, but she faced a couple of nights at the hospital nonetheless. With young children, no family living close by, and a husband unable to get time off of work, she needed help.

People brought food and were generous in offering provisions, the church clergy prayed for the family, and I silently stood by and anxiously waited to see which—if any—friends would step up to help care for her kids.

I love her children dearly. However, I was hoping someone else would jump in and offer to take care of her kids, giving me an excuse not to. I preferred to keep my time for myself. In my weak defense, I already had my own kids and work was throwing urgent project deadlines at me that week while I attempted to work from home. My in-laws were also scheduled to visit that weekend, and the house was the victim of a rather impressive toy and laundry assault highly coordinated by my honey-badger children.

These are just the excuses I can remember. At the time, I'm sure

I had a whole arsenal of them ready to fire in order to get out of *having* to help. So I held off as long as I felt a decent human being could.

However, after some inward debate (read: a debate with the Holy Spirit), like the good friend I knew I *should* be, I offered to have her kids come over to my house to play, eat, and even spend the night if needed.

I could tell my friend was so relieved at the offer and quickly accepted for them a long playdate at my house. As I picked up her children, my anxiety level skyrocketed as images of my work project and bomb site of a home flashed across my mind. I pondered what I could entertain all the kids with—hers and my own—that would keep them occupied for a decent amount of time while I handled the grown-up things on my to-do list.

I put on a movie and quickly got to work picking up dirty clothes off the floor and starting a load of laundry. Within minutes, the two youngest of our kids scampered in begging for snacks . . . right after they had eaten breakfast. Because of course they were hungry for snacks. Why are kids *always* hungry?

After tossing snacks their way, I moved to my computer. I stood at my kitchen counter with my laptop open and mindlessly did dishes as I read through emails.

Then the older kids tramped in needing help opening the water-color trays and paint brushes they'd found—strategically hidden away—in a closet. Oh, and they couldn't find any blank paper. So I stopped the dishes and emails, found the paper, opened the paints, grabbed all the paper towels in the house (just in case), and cleared a space for them to work.

The morning continued in a similar way, with requests that I paint, sing, dance, and play outside with them myself. Eventually, I threw up the white flag. They won. They needed, even wanted, me to be with them.

So I shoved the unfolded laundry into a corner of my bedroom, turned off my email, shut my laptop, and met them all out in the driveway to ride bikes.

And wouldn't you know it? I ended up having the best time hanging out for the rest of the day. We rode bikes, did gymnastics in the yard, created artistic masterpieces with chalk in the driveway, then moved back in to our Picasso-like watercolors.

At the end of the day, after my friend's husband came to pick up their kids, I sat down (albeit for only a minute or two before bedtime chaos ensued) and thought about the reasons I had been so anxious about offering my help and time.

My reasons for hesitating to help my friend boiled down to one thing: I viewed *my* time, energy, and family needs as more important than hers. Specifically, my work was (still is) important to me. That day, I definitely felt it was more important than painting, crafts, and games with a big group of children.

> *We are not holier than anyone else. We are not set apart from them. It's not us and Jesus versus them. We cannot be fooled into thinking this, for even a second.*

I had forgotten something so crucial about living this whole and holy life. Our fellow believers—coworkers, family, whoever—are not set apart from us; they are set apart with us.

I had forgotten that the activities of that day represented quality time with my friend's kids, my own kids—all of them God's kids. I felt my energy was better spent on my own needs and desires.

Ouch. This is so embarrassing to admit. I like to view myself as a nice person, but I can't deny that I tend to set myself and my time and energy a little higher on the ladder of importance than others.

Yet, I'm not more important. My time and energy are not either. The time God allowed me that day was not more limited, more important, or holier than my friend's or her kids'. Not by a long shot.

## A Bigger Purpose

Maybe this "loving one another" as Jesus commanded doesn't look like physically loving on and spending time with someone else like in my situation, but maybe it stems from what we talked about in chapter 3. Maybe it starts with our thoughts and the words we speak.

> Therefore, having put away falsehood, let each one
> of you speak the truth with his neighbor, for we
> are members one of another. (Ephesians 4:25)

To be honest, I've paid minimal attention to this verse in the past, but when I reread it recently, the last half caught my attention.

"For we are members one of another." This suggests we are one. We know from Scripture that, as believers, we are all part of the same body.

> So in Christ we, though many, form one body,
> and each member belongs to all the others.
> (Romans 12:5 NIV)

The right hand is not better than the left, nor is the left better than the right. Different, yes. Is one stronger than another? Sometimes. When one is stronger than the other, it picks up the slack where the other can't.

This is how Christ created the church.

We are not holier than anyone else. We are not set apart from them. It's not us and Jesus versus them. We cannot be fooled into thinking this, for even a second.

Because we are all whole and holy together, we need to remember that we are called to love one another, just as Christ loved us. Our fellow believers are not set apart from us, but with us.

So people must be our purpose.

People equal purpose. Period.

Not our jobs, not our bank accounts, not even good things like being involved in our churches or communities are our purpose. We can be involved with our church, be smart or generous with our bank account, and still not be people driven.

There are some of us who work hard at our jobs to provide for our families so we can live in nice houses, in nice neighborhoods, with nice cars and neighbors. But we're more worried about whether our homes look beautiful enough for HGTV rather than whether they offer comfortable and safe places for our people (and others!) to be.

There are others of us who join a church because it makes us feel good every Sunday. But we stay away from inner-city or global mission trips the church hosts because it's just too hard to see and ultimately connect with people in more difficult situations—the difficulty ultimately set by our own standards of how people should live.

We write a monthly check to our local homeless shelter or food bank because we need to be charitable (tax write-offs, anyone?), but we never make it downtown to cover the homeless with warm blankets or scoop a hot meal into a hungry person's empty bowl.

These are hard truths that I am so guilty of. It's just easier to write a check or scoot into the back pew on Sundays than really engage with people around us or those who need us. And I crave for my home to look like it was recently on an episode of *Fixer Upper*, not because I want to make a comfortable place for my people, but because I want to make it pretty.

*Genuine holiness is when we look not only at how we (or our kids and immediate families) are doing in our zone but also at the needs of others that we can share in. This is different from the perspective the rest of our world has.*

In Ephesians 4:28, Jesus sends a sharp stab of conviction right into my gut.

> Let the thief no longer steal, but rather let him labor, doing honest work with his own hands, so that he may have something to share with anyone in need.

"Let the thief no longer steal . . . doing honest work . . . so that he may have something to share."

Yow. Not going to lie; this verse hurt my feelings. But it is justified. When I ignore the needs of others, I'm ultimately stealing from them—and therefore from God.

I'm stealing relationships, peace, possible joy, definitely love, and God's opportunity to bless them through me.

In my hesitation to watch her kids while she was in the hospital, I was stealing peace from my friend. She worried and fretted about the possibility of mothering her children from the hospital bed or her husband needing to take them with him to work. I was also stealing Jesus's opportunity to show up for her through me.

Are there things in your life where you may not be properly prioritizing your own time and energy, even your thoughts, about someone? If so, then "let the thief no longer steal."

Unfortunately, this takes honest work on our behalf for other people.

Once I got honest with myself about why I was hesitant, I was able to work out the details of helping my friend. And ultimately everyone was blessed in the process, even me.

Once we are honest about how and why we may be stealing someone else's needs and replacing them with our own, we can begin to reposition our people-driven-ness (Did I just make up a word? Let's go with it.) back to the top of our priority list.

Christ called us to love one another. But why?

> *To have relationship, we have to give relationship. All types of relationships. This is what we are called to do in Christ.*

People must be our purpose because they are God's priority.

Genuine holiness is when we look not only at how we (or our kids and immediate families) are doing in our zone but also at the needs of others that we can share in. This is different from the perspective the rest of our world has.

I'm not saying we have to join the next mission trip or donate our entire next paycheck, but I believe God is saying we must first think of other people's needs before we think of our own. We must increase our people-driven-ness.

I also want to be clear that I am not saying we should sacrifice the people God has put in our families and place other people in front of them. There are so many opportunities, like in my situation, where my family would not have to sacrifice at all, but I still hesitated.

It's a balancing game. Your family is your number-one priority and the one you've been entrusted to care for and love.

But God's family (that's everyone else) is a close second. Together, our people and God's people are our purpose.

Sometimes we may not recognize that this holier-than-thou

attitude is even present. Because I, as well as many others, am a master of self-justification. I normalize this attitude, and I am used to seeing and hearing it, so I don't even think twice when I do this.

We justify our own selfishness.

But here's the truth bomb for you, and it's one you already know. This bomb may seem to come out of nowhere, but it's going to clear away the rubble and expose a truth we can't afford to miss.

To have a friend, we have to be a friend. To have relationship, we have to give relationship. All types of relationships. This is what we are called to do in Christ.

This means making time and creating space for people—not only physical time and space but also the emotional time and space it takes to care for, tend to, and be with a friend in need. It also includes making time for the people who are important to that friend. People like my friend's kids.

> Greater love has no one than this, that someone
> lay down his life for his friends. (John 15:13)

As we sail through life, relationships fall away. This is natural and normal . . . here on earth. But that doesn't mean it's OK. Remember, we are living a holy life now, one not like others here before eternity.

So I urge you to take a closer look at why this may be happening. Is it because *we* are the ones too busy with work, hobbies, or watching our favorite TV show to be with, care for, or connect with someone in need? Or maybe we aren't worried about current relationships but instead are always wanting to connect with new ones.

Sometimes we refuse to adjust our thinking, or we let the busyness of schedules slide to a place without white space for relationship. You would think the people who matter to us would naturally rise to the top of the priority list. After all, what we say are our priorities are actually priorities, right?

Wrong.

We let life get in the way of what should be our real priorities. When we allow regular life to interrupt the correct structure of priorities, we aren't living a life set apart from the rest of the world.

I was more worried about finishing a work project and getting my house clean than making sure my friend's kiddos were taken care of well while her husband worked and she recovered. I worried that my energy level would be zapped and I'd suffer in taking care of myself and my to-do list. I wasn't prioritizing my friend and her people. I wasn't prioritizing people at all, other than myself. I know I would have been so grateful for someone to sacrifice her own agenda had the tables been turned and I was the one in need.

When I think of what it means in our culture to be holier than thou, I tend to think of someone who acts self-righteously. Although I think a holier-than-thou attitude doesn't always have to look as negative as self-righteousness, the holier-than-thou person can resemble someone who, like myself, is simply more focused on herself and her own day-to-day than others.

I don't think I'm the only one who does this either. I can't be.

Either way, I feel Jesus sometimes needs us to call this sin what it is if we're going to truly live a whole and holy life. It's the holier-than-thou or more-important-than-thou attitude we view as OK, even justifiable. It's an attitude we do not have authority to claim.

Of course we can claim holiness over our own lives because of Jesus, but God is the only one who can be holier than thou in the lives of the people around us.

We will not be the ones sitting on the judgment throne at the end of this parade. We have authority only over our own lives and can claim His holiness only for ourselves. That's as far as we can go. We must not apply our judgment over to other people.

> "Do not judge, or you too will be judged. For in the same way you judge others, you will be judged, and with the measure you use, it will be measured to you." (Matthew 7:1-2 NIV)

We all know this verse, and we know we're not supposed to judge. But I don't think judgment has to always look like gossip or even negative thoughts about other people.

It can be us thinking about, well, *us*. Thinking first and foremost about ourselves.

There are only so many hours in the day, and our weeks are already filled up with work, our own kids' needs, and a zillion other things for our own families and selves. Our own families need our attention first, work won't wait, or we already had plans for this certain thing for some time, so we can't. Also, we're a little under the weather or aren't able to accommodate that person for any number of other reasons.

My behavior when my friend needed help is just one example of a holier-than-thou perspective that sometimes creeps in when we look around and outside our immediate circle of life. There are a lot of other examples too.

*We cannot be fooled into thinking that we are better than nonbelievers just because they do not think like us.*

Want to know something cool that happened?

For the couple of days after my friend's kids left my house, my own children were happier and, quite frankly, played out. They weren't as needy for my attention as they normally were and holed up in front of the TV or in their rooms playing or reading quietly by themselves.

Because of this and because I had an entire afternoon off from work, I also was re-energized and able to quickly and efficiently finish my project well ahead of deadline, which in turn gave me time to finish cleaning the house.

God blessed me in my giving of myself in that situation. The joke was on me. He loved on all of us a little extra because I chose to love on my friend.

We are called to love one another, just as Christ loved us. If we want Christ to love on us, we must love on Him. This means loving on and being a friend to His people.

> My command is this: Love each other as I have loved you. Greater love has no one than this: to lay down one's life for one's friends. You are my friends if you do what I command.
> (John 15:12-14 NIV)

## Alongside Prebelievers

We know that fellow believers are set apart with us, right? Well, what about everyone else?

Unless we hole up like hermits, we will also encounter people who are nonbelievers. Heck, we encounter them when turning on the television.

We have a unique opportunity to set an example of what it looks like for everyone—not just other believers—to live a whole and holy life. BUT . . .

We cannot be fooled into thinking that we are better than non-believers just because they do not think like us. We are not. We are sinners, just like they are. We need Christ just as much as they do. They are no different from us, except in our knowledge of where we are spending eternity. This knowledge and belief in Christ is the only thing that makes us not better than but better *off* than nonbelievers.

We have Jesus, the One who makes us holy. It has nothing to do with us, so we are not better inherently; rather, we are on level playing ground with everyone. It's as we recognize how much Jesus loves us that we begin to want to love others in the same way.

As we love others—both believers and nonbelievers—we cannot always expect nonbelievers to think or act like we think they should. Just because *we* know and follow Jesus and strive for all that is good, whole, and holy doesn't mean they know or do this for themselves. How can they? There is not a set of holy values they've grabbed ahold of like you and me.

Before moving into ministry work at my church, I worked for years in a corporate setting where the principles of "how things are" spanned light years from what I've come to know as God's original design for the way the world is supposed to be. I worked in sales too. Double ouch. I didn't recognize or understand how different these corporate principles were because I didn't know any better.

Non-Christians work and live from a completely different foundation than Christ followers. Depending on whether they have any type of religion or beliefs at all, life could be fair game for them. They don't have the same set of boundaries, rules, or examples to follow that you and I have in Jesus.

If I'm completely honest with you, only in very recent years have I run hard in Jesus's direction. So I still acutely remember and am easily tempted to slip back toward this prebeliever life. I want to focus on staying inside my own lane while working and living life, not looking to the needs of the coworkers and neighbors around me.

Maybe you're with me, or maybe you've been a Christ follower for years and don't easily get wrapped up in your old worldviews. Or maybe you, also like me, even have nonbelievers in your immediate or extended family and are forced to tolerate their unbelieving ways ... because family, duh. We are forced to live with them. (Please read that last part with all the drip of sarcasm I intended.)

I'm going to make an assumption in saying that, as mothers, we probably hold the most amount of influence in our home. But what about everywhere else? What about in the corporate office? What about at our kids' public schools or practice fields? What about in our regular Monday-night yoga class or at the hair and nail salon?

Most of us work and live with, for, and next to men and women who aren't actively following Christ. I currently live in the South, where there's a church on every corner and Jesus is name-dropped all day long. It's easy to be a "Christian" here because it seems like everyone is on Team Jesus.

But I've lived and visited plenty of places where it's strange to hear people reference Jesus in regular conversation. Even here in Tennessee when I worked in corporate America, Jesus wasn't a regular topic of water-cooler gossip.

Because many people didn't know much about Him.

So depending on which part of the country we live in, where we work, and a number of other factors, we can probably for the sake of argument go ahead and assume that most everyone we encounter does not actively follow and worship Jesus.

I love how my friend Becky Kopitzke, author of the book *Generous Love*, calls them "prebelievers." She takes the position of believing that these children of God have simply not had or taken the opportunity to meet Jesus and follow Him yet.[1]

Just because prebelievers don't follow Christ, hardly or maybe ever, doesn't mean they don't deserve our love and respect. They were created in God's image too, even if they don't know so. Becky's view of them leaves me feeling refreshed. I was a prebeliever for most of my life, even when I still identified myself as Christian.

I believe many of us call ourselves Christians, because, well, we were raised to. We believe there is a God but lack a real relationship with Jesus. And watch out, because I'm about ready to rant like a passionate preacher. So many of us lack knowledge and peace and, therefore, don't realize that we are able to live the whole and holy life ordained for us. And we can live it here on earth prior to our eternity in heaven as rescued children.

Things of this world, like those listed in Galatians 5:19-21, which we talked about in chapter 3, should be expected from anyone not actively chasing after Christ the way we are. Remember these?

> Now the works of the flesh are evident: sexual immorality, impurity, sensuality, idolatry, sorcery, enmity, strife, jealousy, fits of anger, rivalries, dissensions, divisions, envy, drunkenness, orgies, and things like these. (Galatians 5:19-21)

Sure, we may not see this kind of blatant and obvious sin in our everyday lives at our kids' baseball games or in the break room at work—thank You, Jesus!—but we do see strife, fits of anger, divisions, and envy. They may be less overt, like a whispered gossip here and a snarky glance there. (Or not. I've seen plenty of YouTube videos of angry Little League parents.)

Traditionally, American culture has deemed these Galatians 5:19-21 things taboo because of our country's Christian origin, but mainstream America is moving more toward an attitude of acceptance of this kind of sin. "Such things" are becoming more prevalent, not just behind closed doors but out in the open too. We don't blame ourselves.

But Jesus does.

Jesus expects us to live lives worthy of our calling as Christians.

> I therefore, a prisoner for the Lord, urge you to
> walk in a manner worthy of the calling to which
> you have been called. (Ephesians 4:1)

Ephesians 4 discussed unity in the body of believers, but in our society, I think it's worth discussing unity in thoughts of prebelievers, as well.

"But Kristin," you may be saying, "doesn't the Bible say don't be yoked with unbelievers?" Yes, it does. The full verse says,

> Do not be unequally yoked with unbelievers.
> For what partnership has righteousness with
> lawlessness? Or what fellowship has light with
> darkness? (2 Corinthians 6:14)

Can we look at this verse a little closer? While often applied in reference to marriage, I think this verse can apply to any relationship with a prebeliever, as well.

In the original Greek, "unequally yoked" is a compound of both *heteros*, meaning "altered," "strange," or "of uncertain affinity" and *zugos*, which literally means a "beam of balance" that connects two separate scales.[2] A beam that unites two things. In animals, a yoke is used to unite a pair of animals so they can pull together as one.

This Greek definition, coupled with the image of animals yoked, applied to our picture of believers and prebelievers literally shows a balanced beam with two separate scales (that of believer and pre-believer) pulling together as one. Balanced. Equal. One. Stronger together.

But we know this isn't the case. It *can't* be.

As believers, we are set apart with Christ, and anything not holy and set apart cannot be equal, let alone pull together as one.

We are saved, whole, and holy daughters of God, and cannot allow ourselves to be equal and balanced to anything of this world if we want to fully embrace our wholeness and holiness.

In 2 Corinthians 6:14, Paul asked what righteousness and wickedness could have in common and what fellowship light can have with darkness.

Paul is suggesting that light cannot fellowship with darkness. However I personally don't believe that darkness can't fellowship with and move toward light. Light stands its ground. Where light is, darkness disappears. I believe we can interact with, work with, and show love to unbelievers and still not be yoked to them.

Because if we stay yoked to Jesus, He will overshadow any unbelief and darkness.

These prebelievers—the people who see us living our lives differently than they are, differently than most everyone else is—will take notice. It becomes more of an image of us leading them rather than pulling together like animals yoked side by side.

Remember, these people are God's purpose, and this is our opportunity to let them notice Him.

## A Different Station in the Circle

Speaking of noticing and how we view things, the more time goes on, the more I see that my 360-degree view of the world isn't really from the center looking out. It's not me, turning in a circle, looking at all the things and people that touch my life.

It's me looking from the outside in.

Bear with me while I take us back to tenth-grade math. Or maybe it was sixth-grade math for you, and not tenth grade like it was for me. I've never pretended to be good with numbers. Words and reading are more my jam.

If we're talking geometry, the station I view the world from is somewhere in the arc of a circle, staring back toward the center on the radius line. This is a normal viewpoint for us.

Scripture tells us we should have the attitude of Christ and view everything through a Christlike filter, so now that we have and are yoked to Christ, He moves us to the center of His circle, not ours.

If I stood at the center of life with Christ—a holy and set-apart place—I'd look out to a never-ending arc that spreads in all directions, past my own family, work, and community to the entire world. My own life is only in one tiny little spot in that 360-degree view.

We would be able to see and understand the bigger picture. The bigger picture includes everyone and everything else, not just us.

I don't think we'll ever perfectly master this perspective in this life, but we can start. It's one way Christ works on our sanctification.

> Do nothing from selfishness or empty conceit,
> but with humility of mind regard one another as
> more important than yourselves; do not merely
> look out for your own personal interests, but
> also for the interests of others. Have this attitude
> in yourselves which was also in Christ Jesus.
> (Philippians 2:3-5 NASB)

Yes, Jesus has called us to love our families and the people in our own little sphere of influence. But He also calls us to have a holy love and attitude, not a holier-than-thou one, toward all others.

Otherwise we can find ourselves as thieves, stealing peace, love,

and friendship from God's people and ultimately a holy contentment in our relationship with other people.

> Let the thief no longer steal, but rather let him
> labor, doing honest work with his own hands,
> so that he may have something to share with
> anyone in need. (Ephesians 4:28)

## Notes

1. Becky Kopitzke, *Generous Love: Discover the Joy of Living Others First* (Bloomington, MN: Bethany House, 2018).

2. Strong's Concordance, s.v. 2086. heterozugeó, Bible Hub, https://biblehub.com/greek/2086.htm.

# CHAPTER 5

# Raving Fans

## Living Despite Expectations

We've talked about some pretty serious stuff, like the mental games we play with ourselves and even comparison and selfishness. I promise I'm not always so Debbie Downer, friend. Actually, hardly ever.

So let's talk about something lighthearted.

Cheerleading.

Did you smile or groan when you read that? I did both, actually.

I know, I know . . . I gave you a lesson in cheerleading muscle memory already, but years away from the activity hasn't diminished the lessons I gleaned from years of shaking pom-poms. So let me fill you in on how cheerleading summer camps taught me about business, happy customers, and meeting and exceeding expectations.

## Give More to Get More

We were in south Texas in late May, sprawled out across an open field we called "the frying pan" due to its hot temperature and lack of shade. Roughly three hundred college cheerleaders, male and female, from across the southwest region gathered for our company's annual "work week"—five days of intense staff training before our managers released us for a summer-long string of cheer camps. This company runs and sponsors cheerleading camps all across the country, even the world, hiring broke college kids—like me—each summer as the cheer camp instructors.

The sun beat down as we took a much-needed break from the physical portion of our training to take notes on the administrative and logistical side of camp. We learned about the paperwork, payments and payroll, medical release procedures, how to check into camp locations, and so on.

Then our regional manager stood on a collapsible wooden stage with a microphone in hand and told us something I will never forget. "This summer we're going to create not just fans but *raving* fans."

He had recently read the book *Raving Fans* by Kevin Blanchard and Sheldon Bowles and had decided to change the way he trained his staff in order to create raving fans in the cheerleaders and coaches we served all summer long.

It's a simple idea, actually.

Fans are the people who follow, admire, and love someone or something. But add the word *raving* as an adjective, and you've got someone who follows, admires, loves, AND speaks with wild enthusiasm and extreme praise.

In business, this enthusiasm and praise is key. It's what gets your customers to keep coming back, plus it's what gets those customers to get others to come to you. These customers are such fans they wildly rant and rave for others to hear about your great product or service. They answer questions and share stories with others about their experience with your business. And you know what they say: the best form of marketing is word of mouth.

The goal for summer-camp instructors was to get those coaches and cheerleaders raving about their camp experience and us (the instructors), not only to keep them coming back but also to get other teams to join in the following week or semester or even the following year.

This company's product was unique. Usually people attend a camp to gain experience or knowledge—something internal—rather than a tangible product in hand upon departure. So in this particular summer job, the people running the camp *were* the product in a sense. We were a type of service to the coaches and cheerleaders. We, as the camp instructors with all the knowledge and ability to teach and coach, were considered a *product* of our company.

So—in my mind—in order to create fans of the offered product, we had to also create fans of ourselves. Of course, to start with, we did this by doing our jobs. We offered participants what they paid for, which was good, quality instruction.

However, to get *raving* fans, we had to go above and beyond just delivering the base product. We had to go the extra mile and give the customers something they were not expecting.

At cheer camp, coaches expect the staff to teach a new dance to their team, but they don't expect the staff to spend their lunch or dinner break perfecting and critiquing the moves of each camper so they are extraconfident in their performance. Coaches expect the staff to interact with their cheerleaders, but they don't expect them to befriend the athletes and get to know them on a personal level. Coaches expect their teams to come away from camp with a better knowledge of how to cheer, but they don't necessarily expect them to come away from camp with a better understanding of how to be leaders in their schools.

That first summer I learned about raving fans was twenty-ish years ago (Lord, have mercy!), but the initiative is still intact at most

cheerleading summer camps today. Coaches who bring their cheerleaders to camp have the opportunity to give a shout-out to certain
staffers whom they are raving fans of by turning in little "raving-fan"
sheets to the camp's head instructor. I know hundreds of instructors who have gone above the call of duty and created raving fans in
coaches and cheerleaders across the country. I know this because,
when I moved into a managerial role, I saw those coaches request the
same summer camp instructors year after year.

I still remember what it felt like the first time I heard someone
rave about her experience with *me* as her camp instructor.

I had exceeded someone's expectations, and it felt good. I craved
more of it, so I worked hard to get more raving fans.

These were the things I learned sitting in the frying pan:

1. Whatever was expected of me, I would do *more*.
2. With *more*, I could and *would* create fans who raved.
3. Raving turns fans from people who admire me internally to
   praising me externally.
4. That external praise brought and gave me more in the
   long run—more confidence, more recognition, even more
   money and responsibility.

More, more, more.
To get more, I ultimately had to give more.

> *It's hard to enjoy the behind-the-scenes of*
> *our own lives while we are looking out at the*
> *highlight reel of the rest of the world.*

Eventually, my quest to accumulate raving fans through hard
work caught the attention of not just the customers but my managers

as well. Throughout the years working summer camps, I was promoted from camp instructor to head instructor, and I eventually worked my way up to a full-time job in the company's corporate office upon graduation.

This was all great. I believe that hard work deserves payoffs and that to get what you want, you need to work for it. My hard work in the cheerleading industry is something I'm proud of and will always fondly look back on.

However, I built my entire work existence by layering raving fan on top of raving fan. Yes, it was my job, and at work we had requirements and expectations to meet, but the core of the motivation for my work was pleasing other people by doing whatever it took to make them happy and raving about me.

I worked to place exceeded expectation on top of exceeded expectation, and what used to be a fun, lighthearted activity and summer job eventually got heavy. Exceeding expectations became the expectation.

I'm still wired this way. I still strive to fulfill expectations and exceed them whenever possible.

But what happens when I cannot exceed *already* exceeded expectations of others?

Worse yet, what about when I don't exceed or even meet my *own* expectations?

Ugh—there's a can of worms that just spilled everywhere, didn't it? So let's sweep those slimy, slithering expectations back into the can and slap on the lid, shall we?

## Get Real

I don't know about you, but there is little else in my life that feels heavier to carry or makes me feel more sluggish than expectations.

Depending on what is happening in your life at any given time, the weight can be crushing, making it hard to focus or, in extreme cases, even breathe. Our society makes it even worse with the onset of social media, commercials, reality TV (that's *not* so real), royal weddings, magazine covers . . . you name it.

It's hard to enjoy the behind-the-scenes of our own lives while we are looking out at the highlight reel of the rest of the world.

We have kids to feed and clothe, spouses to please, aging parents to visit or take care of, projects due, customers to reach out to, pets to walk, laundry to fold, counters to wipe, blogs to read, shows to watch, and beds to make. All the while, we're "supposed to" look good and be joyful doing it.

I don't think so.

It's time to get real. We can't carry all this and look good and be happy while doing it. Maybe sometimes we can, but not all the time. If we're trying to carry these expectations—whether placed by ourselves or others—we're going to get weighed down.

People cope with the load of expectations in different ways. Some people drink to take the sharp edge off, some people eat when stressed, and some people—like me—retreat to their rooms to lie down, stare at the ceiling, and pray nobody will find them there . . . ever.

There are healthy and unhealthy ways to cope with expectations, but I would say that the only way to positively begin to deal with expectations is, first, know where the weight comes from.

Realistic expectations are fine, great even. They motivate us and get us going. They are the push we need to get things done. However, *unrealistic* expectations are a wall we feel forced to climb. It's their unrealistic scope that adds the heavy weight on us.

Imagine bricklayers tossing bricks to one another as they build a wall, each brick an expectation placed on us by ourselves or others. A smooth toss and a catcher who's ready and willing can streamline the process of building. But an extra-heavy brick or a catcher who isn't quite ready for another one creates an awkward fumble or even a drop.

The moment of impact between reality and unmet expectations can shatter us, causing us to drop what we're holding. It hurts our motivation, our pride, and our contentment. When we expect more than what is realistic, we set ourselves up for failure.

I'm not talking about big goals and dreams here—that's for a later chapter. I am talking about the small, gritty expectations that grind into daily life. For example, the expectation that we'll have a home-cooked meal on the table every night and sit together as a family. Or the expectation that our children should be able to leave preschool property without stripping shirts off and yelling all the way down the hall. The expectation that we should be able to shave our legs in the shower just once in our lives without running out of shaving cream because our spouse or kids used it to shave or decorate the walls.

Or insert whatever perception you have of others' reality. Those examples above are just ones from my current stage of life.

These are the expectations that as moms we assume are normal and realistic for most people. So we expect them for ourselves too. I'll be honest—I don't expect most people's children to take off their clothes in preschool hallways, and I expect most women don't run out of shaving cream every time they try to shave their legs. I assume those are normal expectations for others.

When these expectations aren't met, then we—to say the least—aren't happy.

And if mama ain't happy, ain't nobody happy.

So we have to get realistic.

Would we set unrealistic expectations on our kids or spouses if we knew they would not hit the mark?

No, because we love them and want them to succeed. We want them to go above and beyond what is expected. We need to do the same for ourselves.

My friend Kimberly used to work with middle school girls at her church. She explained to me about a lesson she once taught about "missing the mark," which she adapted from Dannah Gresh's book *Secret Keeper*.[1] Kimberly used the illustration of a target where the bull's-eye is the intended mark. She said to the girls,

> You aim for the mark as closely as you can, because that's the goal. But sometimes, or a lot of times, you miss. Sometimes you miss small, barely skimming the center, and other times you miss huge or don't even hit the target.
>
> The bull's-eye is God's perfection. The Hebrew word for sin can be translated as "missing the mark." We can use the Bible and the Ten Commandments to guide us in aiming for the center, but sometimes we miss. But if we know what the goal is, we can aim as closely as we can to the center of the bull's-eye. That's where the phrase "aim small, miss small" comes from. By knowing the Bible and guidelines for a godly life, we can have a better focus on where we need to aim. But we lust, we lie, we have fits of anger, and we miss the mark.
>
> As humans, we will totally miss the mark on our own, but Jesus bridges the gap for us when we fail.

> In Him, we can hit the bull's-eye way more often
> than without him.

Kimberly's lesson on sin made me think of our targeted expectations. We aim to hit the bull's-eye of those expectations, but we miss all the time.

I wonder if that's part of the reason why the Pharisees asked Jesus about the greatest commandment in Matthew 22.

Sure, we know because of prior verses they were trying to test Jesus, but I wonder if the answer was always intended to be written in His Word for us. Maybe the verses are intended to give us a straight, simple, no-nonsense answer on how to get it right and hit the mark.

> "Teacher, which is the great commandment in
> the Law?" And he said to him, "You shall love
> the Lord your God with all your heart and with
> all your soul and with all your mind. This is the
> great and first commandment. And a second is
> like it: You shall love your neighbor *as yourself*."
> (Matthew 22:36-39, emphasis mine)

Both of these commandments are about relationships—love God, love others.

However, the "as yourself" part sometimes trips me up. It feels weird, selfish, even un-Christian to love myself, especially as someone who has a family to care for and things to do. But we need to remember that we are not only to care for and love others; we also must do the same for ourselves.

God doesn't expect us *not* to love ourselves. In fact, I would venture to say, based on Paul's words in 1 Corinthians, that God expects—even requires—us to love and care for ourselves, as our bodies are not our own anymore but temples of the Holy Spirit. (See 1 Corinthians 6:19-20.) Paul goes on to say in 1 Corinthians 12 that we are all members of one body, and so we are to love both ourselves and others.

Sure, selfishness is the root of most evil, but there's no denying that as humans we have an instinctive, even primal, need to care for and love on ourselves.

So let's love on ourselves in the expectations department, just as we would love our kids, our spouses, our best friends.

We must not set unrealistic expectations that easily set us up for failure and disappointment.

When we are disappointed in ourselves, unhappy and upset because we missed the mark, we absolutely will be primed to not enjoy anything . . . especially the regular routine of life.

The behind-the-scenes moments of our lives that I mentioned earlier will remind us how we're not living up to par.

Want to know why else we shouldn't have unrealistic expectations of ourselves? Because Jesus doesn't.

Wait . . . what? Jesus doesn't expect too much from us, you ask?

Nope. His grace and mercy are proof of that. And that's the best news I've heard.

## Cleanliness Is Next to Godliness

I have a legit question. A question that tackles my claim that we are whole and holy in Christ. It throws in an extra jab to the ribs, just for good measure.

If I can barely manage my life, how can I be godly?

There are so many demands in each day, and I'm simply trying to keep up.

We've often heard the phrase "cleanliness is next to godliness," a maxim used to promote personal hygiene. Cleanliness also represents spiritual goodness and purity.

Maybe it's why it's customary to clean up for church.

Maybe it's even why we try to clean up everything in our lives. Or at least make it *look* like we're squeaky clean.

I confess that I've felt the pressure to be the "it" girl with a beautifully polished house, body, and kids. And I confess that I've not only felt the pressure, but I've taken it on as my own and worked to create that reality for my family and myself.

I've done this with the tangible portions of my life, such as keeping my house clean and my kids' faces washed—both of which I've given up on recently—and I've worked to do this on a spiritual level.

I've signed my kids up for VBS, taught them how to pray, registered my husband and me for Christian marriage events, prayed circles around my family members, and even purchased special matching Easter outfits as a family to complete the pretty picture. (Turquoise was our color this past year.)

Surely our squeaky-clean image lines us up nicely enough to be considered godly. Surely because we look the part, we *are* the part. We are the walking and talking epitome of goodness and purity, right?

As moms we have the challenge of keeping an entire household *and* ourselves going, a challenge that eclipses the time for being the spiritual giants we perceive we need to be.

Did you catch that? We feel there is no time *to be* what we perceive we *need* to be. What we see when we look around, at our own lives and the lives of those around us.

We have these expectations of what it means—or at least looks like—to be a successful, loving, godly mother, so we do the things that clean us up and get us ready to go there.

The truth is this: we don't need a clean house, a clean body, or even clean-cut kids or marriage to come to Jesus.

Remember how we talked about nothing unclean could be in the presence of God in the Tabernacle? That's because God is so holy and pure, nothing unclean can be near Him or it will perish.

Our reality is not this anymore because of our Savior.

Jesus wiped us clean, so we don't have to.

He doesn't expect us to come to Him with it all figured out. The figuring out is His job. He has, in fact, *already* figured it all out.

When I came back from maternity leave with my first daughter, the transition into work was a little rocky. Not just because I was only six weeks postpartum (and you can imagine all *those* issues), but because the intern who picked up the slack during my leave had a hard time letting go of the job upon my return.

It finally took my boss and me telling him to chill out, that I was back and this was *my* job, not his. He could go back to doing what he was always supposed to do.

I think this is what Jesus says to us when we try to clean up our lives. I can almost hear him saying, "Hey, chill. I got this."

He wants us to sit back and enjoy the party He's throwing. We don't have to get ready for it.

> But God shows his love for us in that while we
> were still sinners, Christ died for us. (Romans 5:8)

## It's a Come-as-You-Are Party

I believe we already have a raving fan in Jesus.

He is our Creator and our biggest cheerleader. He made us exactly how He wanted us to be.

The better news?

We don't have to do anything to hear His raving. We don't have to go the extra mile to earn praise from Him. (Feel free to go back and read the first chapter where we talked about how everything God created was good. Also, reference 1 John 3:1; Zephaniah 3:17; and John 3:16. Or the whole Bible is fine too—whatever you have time for.)

## *When we offer grace, we offer Jesus.*

The beauty of this Raving Fan is this: He doesn't set *any* expectations for us to meet or exceed. Look right here in 1 Samuel to see what I'm talking about.

> He raises up the poor from the dust;
>     he lifts the needy from the ash heap
> to make them sit with princes
>     and inherit a seat of honor.
> For the pillars of the earth are the LORD's,
>     and on them he has set the world.
>                                         (1 Samuel 2:8)

That first lines say He raises us from the dust and picks us up from a heap of ash.

He knows we are nothing more than dust without Him. He is the one who raises us up, who lifts the needy and sits us with royalty.

We can't even get up without Him, and we think we can do and be everything.

If all He expects from us is to love Him and love others, then *why do we expect so much more?*

Why do we expect we can do all the things and be all the places for our families, friends, and coworkers? We can't do it, at least not without losing our joy and letting Him slip out of our reach a little bit. So what if the greatest gift we can give to God, to others, to ourselves is grace. Grace not to live up to expectations—grace-filled expectations.

When we offer grace, we offer Jesus. We offer Jesus to others when we lose our expectations of them, and we offer Him to ourselves when we lose the expectations we place on ourselves.

And He's ready and waiting for us to come as we are so He can pick us up and sit us in a seat of honor.

Did you know that the godliest thing we can do is to pursue God? Because when we do that, others see the results of our time with Him rather than what we perceive they want to see in us.

They may seem to want you to follow them, but they need a caring, loving friend, coworker, or family member who takes her cues from her Creator. And that's worth a whole lot more than cleanliness.

## *Pinterest-Perfect Room Moms*

At the beginning of the school year, my daughter's teacher held a parent meeting in her room where she informed us parents of the rules in her class, what our kids would be learning each nine-week segment, and all other pertinent information we'd need to know as our kids embarked on a new school year.

At the end of the meeting, the teacher asked for volunteers to be room parents.

Nobody made eye contact.

I giggled to myself because just the year before in kindergarten, parents of kids in my daughter's class had to have a vote on which of the numerous volunteers for room parent would be the lucky chosen ones.

Maybe by first grade, parents are worn out. I don't know. Whatever the reasons, we sat in awkward silence. And I tried not to giggle or make eye contact with anyone, especially the teacher.

"I will lock this door and this meeting won't end until I have at least one volunteer."

My eyes widened at her boldness, and I internally giggled again. I knew I was going to like this one, but I also felt the pressure of her very teacherly statement. I didn't want to disappoint her or for her to think I was a bad person because I didn't want to be the room mom.

So I considered the option and silently prayed about it right then and there.

However, I knew that if I had one more thing added to my plate, I would break. I would have loved to jump at the opportunity to help my daughter's teacher that year, especially given how much I admire and appreciate teachers and everything they do for my children. But I was pregnant with my third child due in only a few months, I had a honey-badgeresque toddler at home wearing me out, we were in the process of trying to move, my husband had recently been unable to work due to yet another injury, and then of course I had my own work obligations. Plus, I'm terribly noncrafty.

So I didn't volunteer.

I looked around at the other parents. I saw a woman in scrubs, who looked like she had just left a long shift at the hospital. There was a mom I knew was a busy lawyer in town. One mom had two fussing infant twins strapped to her, one in front and one in back. There was even a military officer sitting in his uniform at his son's tiny desk. Another mom was dressed in yoga pants and tennis shoes. I knew from my daughter that this mom was a busy entrepreneur who was taking care of her elderly and sick parents who had recently moved in with her family.

Every single parent in that room had heavy loads of responsibilities and expectations laid on him or her already.

But this teacher was serious. She really did lock us in there until a few parents offered to split the duties evenly.

I both applauded and wondered about the teacher's tactics. Surely she didn't realize that every single one of us in the room already had approximately one billion things going on. Thinking about room-parent duties weighed me down and elevated my anxiety levels.

*Expectations do not define what makes a good mom. Good moms are the ones who follow their dreams, work hard at whatever they do, love their people well, and give Jesus all the credit and glory along the way.*

Those parents who divided the responsibilities in my daughter's class? They killed it. Our class had the best parties ever. From the outside looking in, they were the quintessential Pinterest-perfect room moms. But the teacher and all the other parents, including me, knew in reality they didn't have the capacity to do it all individually. It just looked like it from the outside. We knew it took multiple parents and plenty of other random volunteers throughout the remainder of the year to get the entire job done. But if you were outside that parent meeting, you would never know it.

This is the part where I give all the high fives and hugs to room parents and teachers. Because after watching those parents rock it that year with their everyday and the responsibilities of helping the teacher with parties, activities, field trips, and so on, I'm exhausted. The two times—OK, fine, the *one* time—I volunteered for a party wore me out.

If you are in public education and/or volunteer your time to your kids' school, major kudos to you. Crafting, administrating, and being around kids—more than I already have to—does not fall into the realm of my spiritual gifts.

I want it to be, but it's not.

And if I'm honest with myself, I only *want* it to be because I think it *should* be.

How's that for a confession and conviction?

It's what all the good moms do, right? The Pinterest-perfect moms. They volunteer as room mom and put together goodie bags for each student on the field trip. They know their child's teacher on a first-name basis and can cut up and joke with him or her. They make homemade, wholesome breakfasts, lunches, and dinners every day. They wash behind their kids' ears before church—heck, they wash their kids, period. They have well-thought-out chore charts and systems to help teach their kids proper responsibility.

They are the mamas who do all the things society thinks they should, and they do them well.

I want to be that mama. But my kids hardly ever have their hair brushed, let alone clean, and I hardly ever cook—bring on the drive-through! I can barely remember my kids' teachers' names, and I'm extremely lucky if I make it to field day.

*In the middle of our imperfectness, when we serve Christ in the way we love and forgive— both others and ourselves—we can throw all expectations out the door.*

The picture-perfect mama will never be me. Sure, I can post pictures on Facebook or Instagram that sort of look like me acting as her, but here's the truth: I am not her. What some of these moms enjoy doing, I find pressure in. The Pinterest mom has her way, and it's great. I have my way, and it's also great. The style of life is not what is most important.

I refuse to believe that because I don't meet, let alone exceed, the expectations placed on me by other people, or even myself, that

I'm not a good mom. I also refuse to believe that because you *do* volunteer as room mom or do anything else I listed above, that you aren't either.

Expectations do not define what makes a good mom.

No, I think the good moms are the ones who follow their dreams, work hard at whatever they do, love their people well, and give Jesus all the credit and glory along the way. These are the moms who are doing the thing day in and day out and doing it well.

Even if we eat fast food most days running between lessons or don't fight it when our two-year-old puts on her winter sweater and pants in the summer heat. Even when our kids yell an obscenity as loud as they can at the library because they heard mommy do it the night before or they make a poor choice in who to hang out with after school. Even when we have to enlist childcare and babysitters or other carpooling moms to help with the madness of our schedule.

It's when we can laugh at the shenanigans we endured just to make it to dinnertime that day. It's when we stand up for ourselves and protect our schedules by not saying yes to another thing. It's when we discipline our teenagers or toddlers in an unconventional way for their poor behavior in order to teach them consequences, because maybe unconventional is the only way they'll learn. It's when we lose our minds screaming and yelling but then are able to recognize our own shortcomings and apologize to our families for losing our minds on them.

I think *that's* what makes us good moms.

And not just good moms but *godly* ones. Ones who live a holy life, different from the rest of the world.

And I don't believe the world's expectations of us, or our worldly expectations of ourselves, have any place to sit with us. We are not supposed to do anything with the world and other people as our final motivation. Instead, we can trust in this:

> Whatever you do, work heartily, as for the Lord
> and not for men, knowing that from the Lord
> you will receive the inheritance as your reward.
> You are serving the Lord Christ.
>
> (Colossians 3:23-24)

In the middle of our imperfectness, when we serve Christ in the way we love and forgive—both others and ourselves—we can throw all expectations out the door.

## Note

1. Dannah K. Gresh, *Secret Keeper: The Delicate Power of Modesty* (Chicago: Moody, 2005).

# CHAPTER 6

# Blinders On

## The Art of Knowing Others

As a born-and-raised Kentucky girl, I've always been fascinated with horse racing.

Mint juleps, roses, and oversized Derby hats sing harmony with my love language every first Saturday in May. I have always wanted to own a racehorse, live on a white-picket-fenced farm, and raise up gangly foals to roar around racetracks. There was even a long portion of my childhood when I fantasized jockeying my own horse to the winner's circle.

During my horse racing obsession, I read all the books, took all the riding lessons, and digested every bit of racing knowledge I could in order to learn about the sport. That is where I learned that most jockeys are prohibited from riding their own horses in a race. There went my dream of owning and riding a horse at the same time.

It all came to a head on my tenth birthday when my dad checked me out of school early for a birthday trip to Churchill Downs in Louisville, Kentucky, home of the famous Kentucky Derby horse race. A day at the races with him was—and still to this day is—one of the best birthday presents I've ever received.

I loved everything about it. The white twin spires, the blended smells of hay and leather, and the sound of thundering hooves in loose dirt. I even loved all the obnoxious shouting and bellowing from the tipsy men and women in the stands as they cheered on their two-dollar picks.

My favorite part of the track was the paddock, though. It's the area of the racetrack where you can see the horses up close and personal as their trainers and handlers saddle them and meet up with the riders. This is the part where bettors can get a good look at where to put their money before placing final bets.

At ten years old, I stood entranced as thoroughbreds pranced by right in front of me, setting all my horse-loving senses on fire. If I'd reached out far enough, I could have touched them. I could hear their snorts, see their rippling muscles, even feel their electric energy as they pranced and prepped for the race at hand.

But I couldn't see in their eyes. If one happened to turn its bridled head my way, I could maybe catch a glimpse, but it was over quickly as they pranced on past, shaking their heads.

Their eyes were blocked by small squares of firm leather, called blinders, covering the rear vision of the horse, forcing it to see only in a forward direction.

Because I was deep in the trenches of my horse obsession, I knew the strategy behind this practice of wearing blinders. With eyes on the sides of their heads, horses have peripheral vision, which in racing can cause the animal to run off course should they begin to look around and become distracted. So trainers and jockeys force their racers to focus, keeping them looking down the straight and narrow.

But I still wanted to see their eyes, to at least try to know what they were feeling as they prepped for their next big event. As a ten-year-old little girl, I longed to know these horses, and I imagined some sort of feel-good, fairy-tale connection with them. You know, the kind you would read about in stories about a girl and her horse. *Black Beauty*, anyone?

Please remember, I was ten.

It's kind of funny looking back, because now as a grown adult (most of the time), I'm reminded of this longing for connection when I think about my own life now.

There have been people in my life I've longed to have a closer connection with who never even saw me. Like that one boy in middle school or the director of the choral show I was auditioning for or even the captain of the cheerleading squad. Maybe you know what I'm talking about—people you'd love to get to know better or at the very least have them notice you. But they have blinders on.

Have you ever thought *you* might be the one with the blinders on? Unfortunately, I've been on this side. I know what it's like to be in the shoes (horseshoes?) of someone with blinders on, focused solely on the task at hand and not able to see what or who is around me.

Roughly a year after I started a new job, I walked down the office hallway and heard my name called.

A woman I'd never seen before came scampering up and leapt into a conversation regarding budgets, timelines, and logistics of an upcoming project.

Two thoughts ran through my mind as she jabbered on.

Who the heck is this person? And why is she talking to me like she knows my job?

I had zero clue as to her identity. *None.* Her face didn't even look vaguely familiar. What she talked about was extremely familiar, but who it was coming from was a different story.

Clearly this person was a coworker of some sort because the nature of her conversation and knowledge of the projects my department had in the works was on point. She even referenced conversations she and I had before. Not to mention we were literally standing in the office hallway.

Then—to add more fire to the humiliation pit—she seamlessly slid into asking how my kids were and how Bryant's work had been going since a recent business transition.

This lady *knew* me. Knew my family. Knew my job *and* my husband's job.

And I had no idea who I was talking to.

Luckily, my acting skills were sharp that afternoon, so I played along like we were old friends. But I couldn't get away fast enough to save face.

After narrowly escaping the conversation with my pride intact, I raced over to a coworker and whispered my dilemma.

Laughing at me (definitely not laughing *with* me), my trusted confidant informed me the woman was a director.

A director.

While she worked in a different office location, she and I had had multiple conversations over the phone and by email. So yes, I *did* know, or should have known, this woman. At least the sound of her voice.

We were already Facebook friends too. I about died.

Now, I am the first to admit that I have a terrible memory (thank you, motherhood), but this was mortifying. I should have known this person. In fact, I did know this person, and she knew me.

On the bright side, I think maybe I should have won an Oscar for that performance.

Funny side note, in order to remember this story, I was forced to text my coworker to ask her to remind me exactly how it went down. Shameful, y'all. This memory of mine is shameful. While my memory seems to not be getting better since that day in the office, I need you to know I'm working on it.

Maybe you're not extremely forgetful like I am. Or maybe you're more like my sister—a walking Rolodex of stored information. It's not even fair how many of our memories she is keeping for herself that I never even realized I'd lost.

No matter which side of the memory spectrum you fall on, I think there's a lesson we can and should learn from my embarrassing coworker story.

I had gone through almost an entire year of work with blinders on.

Much like those racehorses at Churchill Downs with blinders on their bridles, for a year I had been so laser focused on my own work and what was happening right in front of me, I didn't even notice the people around me. Even the people directly affected by what I was doing and who affected me.

This coworker not only saw me, she got to know me, checked on me, and even followed up with me about both work and home life.

And I didn't even see her.

I think Satan uses this type of laser focus (which can absolutely be a good thing sometimes) for his own good. He uses these blinders and doesn't allow anything else in our vision that would set us apart from the world. He uses it to conform our focus on self—just like our culture.

He doesn't want us looking at others because that's what Jesus does.

I spent a long time ignorant of this woman and the friendship we could have potentially had because Satan used my blinders to keep me focused only on myself and my own work.

It makes me wonder what or who else is right in front of me that I'm not seeing? What or who are my blinders causing me to miss?

How often do we get so wound up in our work outside and inside the home to really stir up not just a need, but a desire to see and know others? And what about our ingrained desire to be known, as well?

My guess is that this happens extremely often. More often than we'd probably ever admit to ourselves.

But we're on a mission to start living our whole and holy lives in Christ. Lives in which we don't have to give more, but we can get more. Lives where we rip off the blinders that Satan is trying to keep strapped on us so we can see what else is available for us.

I believe a crucial part of holiness is this idea of being known—by God and by other people. However, there are two sides to this. Everything about our world screams self-preservation, self-indulgence, and self-promotion. So naturally, this would lead to a desire to be known by others.

But holiness is something different than that. It also means we need to know others. Part of holiness is striving to be known by others and by God because we know others and know God.

So I want to challenge you, as I challenge myself, to rip the blinders off in our day-to-day.

## A Time and Place for Holy Blinders

In an attempt to stay true to my self-proclaimed horse expertness, I need to point out that racehorses don't keep their racing blinders on all the time. They are allowed the freedom to have them off and walk around to do their regular horsey things. They also don't do all their training with blinders bridled on. They do their daily horse stuff and even do some focused training with full peripheral vision, taking in who and what is around them. This is to help educate them, keep them safe, and even keep their eyes healthy and able to see well.

However, when it's time and necessary, the blinders go on so the horses can focus on their main task at hand without distraction. Horse trainers know the best time and place to have their racehorses focus solely on what's in front of them.

Likewise, in our lives, I don't think having blinders on is always a negative thing. However, it boils down to only allowing the blinders to stay on during certain seasons or times when we *need* them.

So maybe—if looking at racehorses as our example—blinders can be a *good* thing because they keep us from being distracted, keep us safe, keep us healthy.

What if God gives us holy blinders so we can't see and know something or someone is there because it's not ours to know?

*Sometimes we already have better than what we want. Sometimes we ache for relationship but don't look at the ones already established.*

We must ask God for guidance on when holy blinders need to stay on and when worldly blinders need to come off. We need to discern when to focus on what's directly in front of us and when we can walk through daily life with full, holy peripheral vision. My blinders that kept me from even noticing my coworker were self-driven, worldly blinders, and I allowed them to keep me from noticing, even celebrating, serving, or encouraging the wonderful people around me. My blinders kept me from having a godly perspective.

We don't have to go through day-to-day lives blinded to what and who is around us. I think there is a holy time and place for this, but for the most part, we can look around fully and get to know others.

I think this idea of knowing others and being known by others stirs up another level of holiness that will bring us into a deeper relationship not just with people but also with Jesus.

Jesus's mission was to be known as the Son of God, but He also knew others. He knew them in the sense that He knew where they lived, who they were, where they had come from, and what they were like on the inside. We have plenty of people in our lives right now, but are we looking for more relationship farther than we need to?

## Look Around

Have you ever read the Book of Ruth? If you haven't, go ahead. It's short—only four chapters.

If you have read it, you know it centers on Ruth, a Moabite widow. We can learn great things from Ruth: loyalty, selflessness, hard work, and the list goes on. But you want to know who I learned a thing or two from in this story?

Her mother-in-law, Naomi.

Naomi is really only the focus at the beginning and the end of the Book of Ruth, with a tad bit here and there in the middle. But just because the book wasn't named after her, the way it was for Ruth, doesn't mean she isn't a crucial person we can learn a thing or two from.

The beginning of the Book of Ruth introduces us to Elimelech and his wife, Naomi, a nice Jewish couple living in Bethlehem with their two sons. Unfortunately, famine hits the land, so Elimelech packs up his little family and moves to Moab, where they live for a while—long enough to settle in, for the two boys to marry local girls, and for life to be good.

Eventually though, Naomi's husband and both her sons die. She is left in a foreign land with her two daughters-in-law, Ruth and Orpah. Naomi decides she needs to head back to her homeland instead of staying in Moab, and she begs Ruth and Orpah to go back to their homes and find new husbands, explaining that she is too old to provide sons for her daughters-in-law to marry.

Back in biblical times, much of a family's dignity fell onto the shoulders of the male children. Sons were highly coveted because of their ability to carry on family names and traditions. So it was natural Naomi wished for a son, especially since she had lost both of hers. I'm assuming she also longed for a husband too, but I can't be sure. Especially knowing she'd have to learn all over again how to share the covers with a new man, she may have been OK with it.

Anyway, Orpah is easily swayed and hightails it back to her fam in Moab, but Ruth pledges loyalty to Naomi and leaves with her to go back to Bethlehem. After returning home to Bethlehem, Naomi is still unhappy and resentful, so much so that she wanted others to call her Mara, which means "bitter." She wished for a better dealt hand from God.

What she didn't realize, though, was that she already had better. She had Ruth.

Ruth's name means "friend," and she was definitely that to Naomi, plus so much more. Ruth was loyal, hardworking, courageous, obedient, and humble. Naomi had faithfulness and honor radiating from her daughter-in-law, as well as a future foremother of Christ Jesus. Honestly, how much better does it get than that?

This story of Naomi and Ruth makes me look at the things I covet, both material and relational. But it especially makes me take a closer and longer look at the people in my life who are *already* surrounding me, when I keep looking for more.

Sometimes we already have better than what we want.

What relationships do you already have that are better than what you want? Ones that maybe you can really look at and focus more on. Remember, the grass isn't always greener.

Sometimes we ache for relationship but don't look at the ones already established.

While it is holy and good to expand our circles, invite others in, and make new friends or acquaintances, I don't believe we necessarily have to go looking for more relationships all the time.

I think we can get more from those we already have. Naomi certainly did from Ruth.

Take a look around. Look at your kids, your spouse or significant other, your parents, your neighbor, your boss, your subordinate, your barista, your cousins, your nurse or counselor, your children's teacher, your anybody.

Look at the people surrounding you. It doesn't matter what form these people take, they're there.

God has provided relationship for us here on this green earth. Naomi already had Ruth, and, once she finally recognized and saw her blessings through Ruth, she dropped her bitter label. We need to do the same. These people are walking and talking opportunities for us to experience Christ's joy through relationship.

We just don't know it because we don't know them. In order to recognize them for who and what they are, we need to get to know them better—really know them.

Though there's a step we must first take.

If we are going to be holy and whole, we have to first spend time really knowing Jesus. This is a given. We know it's in our best interest to get to know Him better and better.

## To Worship Is to Know

Part of knowing Jesus includes worshipping Him and gravitating to what worship does for us.

That's just the word we tend to use, but don't let it scare you off because the idea of worship means different things to different people. I believe knowing another person intimately and taking the time necessary to do that is a worshipful activity.

The most common form of worship you find in the North American church today is through music.

Beth Moore wrote, "I wonder whether music is something created or if it is something eternal. Something that existed between the Father, Son, and Holy Spirit before God ever said, 'Let there be . . .' "[1]

I think she may be right. Music does have a place in our idea of eternity-oriented worship. We even see it as a part of heavenly worship in John's revelation.

I have zero doubt that we were created to experience and to know music as a form of worship. Music, whether we are musically inclined or not, is woven into how we are built to worship our Creator.

My nine-year-old, McKenna, said to me the other day, "Mom, isn't it weird how when you know a song so well, you can be doing whatever and then all of a sudden catch yourself singing it? And you *didn't even know* you were singing?"

> *I believe it is also a form of worship when we engage in real relationship with other people, because we were also created for relationship, just as we were created for worship.*

I smiled. She was right. I had never noticed, but thinking about her observation, I can recall times when I've been singing or humming and didn't even realize it until someone said something or some other trigger made me aware.

I believe this is how true, pure, and holy worship is. We just do

111

it and don't even realize it; it's something that just happens without effort and is natural.

I believe this brings us back to the natural, whole selves we talked about in chapter 1.

We were created for worship. By definition, worship is the feeling or expression of reverence and adoration. It's not just a feeling but also the *expression* of reverence. So if we were created for worship, we were created to feel and express reverence and adoration.

A common definition for *worship* means to bow down or bend over. It is seen through our posture, with hands up and heads down, bent low to the ground when we pay homage to God. We worship when we sing songs of adoration. We worship when we serve others.

> Therefore, I urge you, brothers and sisters, in
> view of God's mercy, to offer your bodies as a
> living sacrifice, holy and pleasing to God—this
> is your true and proper worship.
> (Romans 12:1 NIV)

If as Romans 12:1 says, true and proper worship requires offering our bodies as living sacrifices, then I am inclined to think that true and proper worship gives us the opportunity to be most like Jesus, since Jesus was a living sacrifice as well.

> *Our entire society is self-seeking and self-*
> *focused, so the only way to be set apart is*
> *to be others-focused.*

So what does worship do for us?

It puts us in a proper and humble position, it elicits emotions, and it brings clarity to what our souls need to fully live a life that is holy and pleasing to God.

It resets our spirits and invites His holiness in, back to our natural and created state of being—one that is fully in tune with our Creator.

I believe it is also a form of worship when we engage in real relationship with other people, because we were also created for relationship, just as we were created for worship.

Introvert, extrovert, ambivert, whatever "vert" you are, God enjoys when His people enjoy, help, and sacrifice for one another. Anytime we step in to ease the burdens or multiply the gifts we know are plaguing or blessing another, we worship—through expression—our God.

> For you were called to freedom, brothers. Only
> do not use your freedom as an opportunity for
> the flesh, but through love serve one another.
> For the whole law is fulfilled in one word: "You
> shall love your neighbor as yourself."
> (Galatians 5:13-14)

The only way to do this on a deep, spiritual, and holy level is to get to know one another.

I'm not talking about simply knowing *of* someone; I mean *really* knowing them. Going beyond their physical existence or what their last Facebook post was, beyond knowing the color of their hair or even the color of their politics.

We need to get to know their quirks, their tics, their details.

## Get Out of Your Own Way

Remember the director from work I didn't recognize? Well, in an effort to redeem myself, I made a point to get to know her a little better. Obviously she knew me, so I felt I at least owed it to her and myself to get to know *her*.

So I sought her out to say hello whenever possible. I asked questions about her kids, paid attention to what she had going on, did some friendly Facebook stalking, and asked her if she needed help with anything she was currently working on.

These little things that we both did added up to a big sum.

Eventually we became friends—good friends. Friends that text to laugh about the stupid things we just did and the goofy things our kids said and to remind each other to tune in to "our show" together. She's the one I can also count on to always tag me in the latest, weirdest, and truthful motherhood memes on social media.

What if I hadn't gotten to know her? What if I never knew that she loved to sing karaoke? What if I never knew that she named her pet after her favorite sports team? What if I never knew her obsession with 1990s hip-hop or spicy tuna rolls with shrimp sauce on the side? What if I never heard or saw her cry over lost babies and loved ones' illnesses and deaths?

All that joy, fun, enlightenment, laughter, and connection would still be sitting on the other side of my ignorance. On the other side of my self-seeking daily grind. On the other side of the firm, leather blinders I wore bridled to my head.

But I got out of my own way and stepped over to the other side of a whole and holy relationship.

One thing I know about living a whole and holy life is that it doesn't look or feel like everyone else's. Our entire society is self-seeking and self-focused, so the only way to be set apart is to be others-focused. We have to go out of our way to do this. We have to rip the blinders off that we've so willingly left on.

I once heard a sermon on taking vacations that stuck with me.

OK, so the sermon wasn't actually about taking vacations. It was about how Jesus did life. But as I sat thinking about all the trips we take, things we do, and so on, I wondered about where we focus and pay attention even while vacationing.

We take vacations on purpose; it's about the destination. We book a trip to the beach because we want to be at the beach. We Google hidden mountain lodges to hole up in because we want to experience all that nature has to offer. We look at the destination and what we'll do when we get there.

But what if we stopped looking at the end point and looked instead at the road map we use to get there? What if on that journey to our destination, we went out of our way to get to know those we are supposed to pass?

Like *really* get to know them? And let them get to know us.

> You are my friends if you do what I command
> you. (John 15:14)

I believe that living a truly whole and holy life includes this. It has to. Over and over again the Bible points back to people and relationships. Verses and passages from Genesis to Revelation discuss the importance of loving and serving one another. The Bible even commands it in Romans 13.

> For the commandments, "You shall not commit
> adultery, You shall not murder, You shall not steal,
> You shall not covet," and any other command-
> ment, are summed up in this word: "You shall love
> your neighbor as yourself." (Romans 13:9)

Our destination—our purpose in life—ultimately boils down to glorifying God and living a life worthy of His calling for us.

Don't miss this part. It's *living* a life worthy. *Living.*

*Living* is an action word, not the end point. It is what and where we are at right now.

It is not what has been done, or will be done, but what is currently happening.

So what if the purpose is not the destination of *having* that friend but the journey of *knowing* that friend? That coworker or neighbor or whoever that person is.

There's no denying Jesus was on a mission with His life. He had a destination: to save the world. We know Jesus was intentional with His life, with His all-night prayer meetings and scheduled Last Supper. He had His own list of to-dos before resurrection day, but I noticed something about Him.

He went out of his way to find people, to get to know them, and to help them. If you have time and the energy to study the geography of Jesus's ministry, you can find multiple episodes of Jesus taking what look like detours to us. But those detours turned out to be the purpose of that route taken to His destination.

Look at Mark 7:31-37, for example. He started in Tyre, and His destination, the Sea of Galilee, was south, but He went north through Sidon instead of immediately going south. He went up and around—miles and miles out of his way—to get to where He was heading.

Why?

Because of people.

He loved and adored people. He had a great reverence for people and loved them. He even fostered relationships when He was not going to benefit from that relationship. He fostered relationships that would take from Him. This is true and holy testament to being a whole and holy friend—doing the hard thing for the benefit of others.

Have you ever seen someone running in negative-twenty-degree snowy weather? Or seen parents taking their preschoolers into Chuck E. Cheese's for a birthday party?

You think they must really love running or whatever that thing is you will never do. And they must really, *really* love their kids to take them into Chuck E. Cheese's for a birthday party. (I'm only sort-of kidding about Chuck E. Cheese's.)

Jesus really loves people, and He goes out of His way for them. In Mark 7, Jesus traveled out of His way to be with, get to know, and heal someone.

Friend, we need to be like Jesus and get out of our way in our daily forward march. We need to look at our road map to this destination of whole and holy living.

This is where we turn knowing others into a form of worship.

The time is now to rip off the blinders we are wearing so we can see the people Jesus has put around us, not just right in front of us.

When we really know people, we live a life filled with whole and holy relationship.

## *N*ote

1. Beth Moore, *Feathers from My Nest: A Mother's Reflections* (Nashville: B&H, 2005), 99.

# CHAPTER 7

# Come Alive

## When Dreams Become Reality

L ast night my family and I had our occasional movie night. While the idea of watching a movie may seem simple to you, at my house it's anything but effortless. It's nearly impossible to sit down as a family and focus for an hour or two without bathroom breaks, sudden hunger, or some type of sibling shenanigans going down.

So if my husband or I want to relax and watch a show, we have to choose one that's kid-friendly, and we have to make a big deal out of it.

A *big* deal.

Movie night prep begins around 4:30 or 5 with premovie dinner. Dinner has to happen early so we can gorge ourselves on popcorn later and kids are full and not easily hangered. *Hanger* is, of course, the verb form of *hangry*.

Pajamas are put on because we never know how long it will take us to finish the movie, and bedtime needs to be the immediate option once the movie is over. My silent prayers are sent up that sleep overcomes the children before the end. (This petition to God is yet to be answered.)

We set a countdown to showtime, and often there is intermission for bathroom breaks because of preschooler-sized bladders. (Read: my own post-three-children mama bladder.)

While popcorn is popping, furniture is moved from the middle of the living room, and blankets, pillows, sleeping bags, and anything else comfy is thrown down and spread out across the floor.

Last night, once everyone was set and ready, we scarfed down popcorn and queued up *The Greatest Showman*.

I'm a total sucker for musicals and still plan to make my grand debut on Broadway someday, so I was excited.

One of the first songs Hugh Jackman belts is called "Come Alive." My ears immediately perked up because I had this exact statement stewing in my heart for the moms I know—come alive.

It was these lyrics right here that stopped me dead in my popcorn chomping.

> When the world becomes a fantasy . . .
> 'Cause you're dreaming with your eyes wide open.

Dreaming with eyes wide open. When dreams become reality.

*That* right there. Yes, *that* is what I want. I want this for myself and for all the mamas I know.

I get swept away daily in the grind—the packing lunches, refereeing fights between siblings, managing emails and meetings, paying medical bills and car notes, searching for that blasted missing sock in the laundry pile—and I don't even recognize that I'm basically sleepwalking through each day. I refuse to believe I'm the only one either.

Sure, I think there are moments, minutes, hours of our days when we are joyful, excited, and living life fully.

But dreaming with our eyes wide open?

That is what I want for you and for me.

That our dreams actually happen in our day-to-day.

Even when we have the regular same ol', same ol' happening around us. Even when we're still working it, wife-ing it, mom-ing it, life-ing it.

Maybe this daily grind could even become a portion of our fantasy.

As the cast danced and sang on the screen, my daughters stood up and started singing at the top of their lungs. They jumped and giggled and pretended they were on stage at the circus too.

Song and dance brought the cast and my daughters (through interpretive dance) alive as we watched *The Greatest Showman*.

And it made me wonder, "What about me?"

*What makes me come alive?*

## *When Did We Stop Dreaming?*

I ask you this question, just as I asked myself.

At what point did we stop daydreaming?

Gosh, when I was young, I had so many crazy dreams. I wanted to ride racehorses in my spare time, I wanted to travel the world at the drop of a hat, I wanted to own a farm and be a veterinarian, and I wanted to travel to Africa and live in a bungalow with my pet cheetah named Duma. I wanted to be a big Broadway star and live the life of a traveling singer and actress.

All of these at the same time.

So when did these dreams shift?

Was it when I received the first real bill that I owed? Was it when I signed the contract on my first job? Was it when a ring was slipped on my finger or I saw double pink lines on the pregnancy test?

Or was it the sum total of all these things?

As I sit here thinking about *The Greatest Showman* and P. T. Barnum's wild and crazy dream of a circus show, I want to give us both permission to dream big again.

My dreams were wild and crazy once upon a time. Now that I'm older, they are practical and safe.

> *I want to get back to a place where I dream big and bold. I think you should too, because that's the sweet spot where our excitement for life meets our pure, whole selves and we come alive.*

I want to be able to retire in comfort financially. I want to go on vacation with my family once or twice a year. I want to be out of debt. I want to enjoy twenty minutes of quiet without being interrupted and not have to share a bite of my dessert with someone else.

Looking at these dreams now, I'm sort of irritated with myself. While great, these seem more safe and tame, more like goals. Should these goals really count as "dreams"?

For one, they don't come close to having the coolness factor my younger dreams held. Yes, I now have a family and responsibilities to take into account when planning and dreaming, but where is the wild and crazy, the big and the bold?

Where is the facet that brings an adrenaline rush or the component just scary enough for my dreams to be wild and crazy? Where is the element that forces me to feel really alive?

I think maybe as we grew up, we hit certain markers that were at least *close* to these dreams, and maybe that's when something shifted.

I may not have lived in an African bungalow with a pet cheetah, but I've traveled to Africa, and I saw a cheetah roaming wild in the Maasai Mara. *Check.*

I may not have ever ridden a racehorse, but I've watched and bet on them from the grandstands. *Check.*

I may not have ever owned a farm or been a vet, but I currently live in the suburbs with a few dogs and chickens in the backyard. *Check.*

But these things I've checked off were never really my dreams. They are closely related to them, but not the exciting dreams of my youth.

I want to get back to a place where I dream big and bold. I think you should too, because that's the sweet spot where our excitement for life meets our pure, whole selves and we come alive. I want to get back to that spot despite barely having time for work and family, and I believe we can. But we're going to have to take a special road to get there.

## At the Corner of Confused and Unsure

Often work-hard mamas struggle thinking about how to come alive.

OK, hold up a second. That sentence was hokey. You probably would never think about it in those exact words. I sound funny even to myself saying, "How should I come alive today?"

Really, what does that even mean?

But it's a valid question I think we should spend some time answering.

What does it mean to come alive? What does it feel like? look like? sound like?

Let's travel into our Bibles to the first psalm:

> He is like a tree
> > planted by streams of water

that yields fruit in its season,
and its leaf does not wither.
In all that he does, he prospers.
The wicked are not so,
but are like chaff that the wind drives away.
(Psalm 1:3-4)

I love this piece of Scripture so much. I've prayed this verse over myself, my husband, and my kids during the first week of school. I've prayed for my kids to stand strong and rooted as they start school and for my husband and me on new business endeavors.

It's the description of what it looks like to thrive. I want my family and me to not just survive, but thrive.

I asked earlier when it was that we stopped dreaming, and I ask a parallel question now.

When did we decide that simply surviving is good enough?

When did it become good enough to just make it through the day, the week, or the month? Or to just make it to the next paycheck, to the next vacation, or past the terrible twos?

When did it become about survival instead of looking for more? Looking for fullness and abundance and truly thriving in this life right now?

Every mom at some point has said to herself, *I just need to make it to naptime* or *to Friday* or *through this phase of preteen hormones.*

It's just survival for so many of us, whether it's dealing with surviving each day of parenting or surviving the work day or quarter.

I want us to push past surviving and live fully thriving.

I believe the first psalm is an appropriate section of Scripture to look at more closely in the discussion of living our lives to a point of thriving.

Psalm 1:3 describes a tree—a healthy one. How do we know a tree is alive and thriving?

Healthy trees stand tall and straight, produce leaves or fruit, root themselves deeper and deeper as they continue growing, and are hard to knock down.

Gosh—doesn't this sound appealing?

If we use this tree in Psalm 1 as a metaphor for our lives, we need to see how we compare. Are we prospering and thriving, producing fruit where we've been planted?

Let's go ahead and assume that, as believers, we're planted by streams of water.

> On the last day of the feast, the great day, Jesus
> stood up and cried out, "If anyone thirsts, let
> him come to me and drink." (John 7:37)

Hint: because Jesus is the One who gives us living water, we are planted near a deep, sustainable source of water. It's important to note that not all people are planted by His water source. Because we are near to Him, we have a deeper, more sustainable source, especially during dry seasons.

So we have our water source—Jesus.

Have you ever seen a tree that throughout a good portion looks healthy but on every few branches or so (maybe even just one), the leaves are brown, withering, and falling off?

To be a complete and *whole* healthy tree, *all* the limbs need to be thriving, not just some.

Are there parts of you that are withering under the pressure of life? Lord, have mercy, there are for me sometimes!

Currently, I'm in the terrible twos with my youngest, Rockie May, and it's been a rough year. Her constant demands and neediness coupled with a lack of vocabulary make each day, well, loud and filled with frustrated screams. (Dear Heavenly Jesus, please rain your mercy down on us during her *threenage* years.)

Rockie May is slightly stubborn (like a donkey) and now has a habit of hitting, pulling, and pushing me (or anyone else) when she doesn't get her way.

My body is physically withered from all the toddler abuse it endures daily.

At the end of a long day with her, all I want to do is crawl into bed and not let anyone touch or talk to me.

I don't want my other girls to snuggle up for hugs, and I definitely don't want to indulge anybody else in any "other" way. (Sorry, husband.)

I feel emotionally and physically withered.

We mamas give out all the time. We plan our kids' school lunches, our work trips, maybe even a family vacation. We pick up kids in our arms, in our cars, and emotionally. We do the thing, day in and day out. The world seems to need everything *from* us.

> *God wants us to live from our pure, whole selves so we cannot portion away the inspiring, creative, I-want-to-do-this aspects of our lives. He built us with a certain set of skills, passions, and creative abilities. It is to our Father's glory that we carry much fruit.*

The tree in the psalm doesn't wither and it bears fruit. In order to not wither, we must put life back into us so we can continue to give of ourselves to our children and others. We're already near our water source, but what about the fruit *we* eat? Not just our home and work life that produces benefits and rewards, but our intrinsic rewards that feed us? The things that fill us up and keep us going.

This fruit doesn't always have to be directly related to other people either. But this fruit that is not related to our kids, families, or even work can and should be seen in us as well. We just need to know how to recognize it.

I know a few ways we can recognize it. It's the human version the Psalm 1 tree holds.

> It sounds like laughter and joyful chatter, peaceful silence, and still air.
> It looks like smiles, movement, and a calm demeanor.
> It feels like energy running through your body and being strong and settled.

There's a peaceful yet energetic current of life that surrounds someone who has "come alive." Do you recognize any of this in yourself ever? If not, it's time to jump-start life and start living.

After a long day of (poorly) parenting my two-year-old, I find peace and even laughter when I sit and write words down in a journal or prayer book. I find movement and calm when I take my dog on a long walk at the dog park. I even find energy when I jump online and begin playing around and building websites. (I know, I'm a total nerd. But I love creating something pretty out of code. I give you full permission to judge me.)

*Why have we let our reality shape our fantasy?*
*We need to let our God-driven fantasies shape*
*our realities.*

God wants us to live from our pure, whole selves so we cannot portion away the inspiring, creative, I-want-to-do-this aspects of our lives. He built us with a certain set of skills, passions, and creative abilities.

It is to our Father's glory that we carry much fruit, both what

He's provided for us and what we're providing for Him and others. God is in the profession of bearing and carrying much fruit.

> "By this my Father is glorified, that you bear
> much fruit and so prove to be my disciples."
> (John 15:8)

He wants you and me to do the same.

What's that trip you've been wanting to take? That painting class? That new Etsy shop, or even a college degree in something more interesting to you? What makes you dream big and start planning to do something inspiring, creative, and outrageous for you?

Think about these things, and think about your skills, passions, and abilities. Once we begin thinking, we begin dreaming with our eyes wide open.

## To-Do Versus Want-To-Do

I jumped on Facebook to ask friends about these questions, their own desires and dreams, just to see what they would say and if they do anything to come alive.

It's funny, the answers I received were not what I was expecting. I thought I'd have friends tell inspiring and creative stories or tidbits about how they really live and enjoy life.

But their answers were more geared to what they do in order to get motivated to get things done that are on their to-do lists, not their *want*-to-do lists.

Answers included putting on motivating and upbeat music to fold laundry or searching YouTube for mommy hacks. This wasn't what I wanted to know. Not even close. However, the fact that my friends answered this way confirmed that moms have a hard time thinking past the ever-present to-dos in our lives.

What in the world? This makes me frustrated for all of us.

Why have we let our reality shape our fantasy? We need to let our God-driven fantasies shape our realities. We deserve more than to simply do our to-dos. We deserve to do our want-to-dos when God lays them on our hearts. When He lays a desire on our hearts, I have full confidence that He will equip us to fulfill it because the desires are within God's will for us.

> And the king granted me what I asked, for the good
> hand of my God was upon me. (Nehemiah 2:8)

We were created for joy and laughter and adrenaline rushes.

We were created to do and be certain people. To do and be more than what needs to be checked off our list. We are meant to be set apart, people who love, live for, and worship a good God.

You've probably already figured out that I'm a list maker. I'll sometimes make a list of things I've already done, just to get that satisfied feeling of checking them off.

But right now, we're going to make a new list.

Don't worry; our regular work and life checklists will be waiting for us when we get back. Unless you know how to make laundry disappear for good. If you do, then please send me an email ASAP. I would be more than happy if laundry was permanently checked off.

On this new list, I want us to list the things that we don't *have* to do but that we *want* to do. Sure, we want to take care of our children, but if we're being completely honest, we also have to do that.

I want you to think beyond responsibilities and into blessings.

Having trouble thinking of something?

Here's my best tip. Pretend you're ten years old again. What was it that you *wanted* more than anything? What was it you wanted to *do* more than anything? What was it you wanted to *be* more than anything? What did you picture your future looking like?

Grab a piece of paper and jot down some notes. What were the things you loved to do and play?

These things you wrote down may give you insight into where you might find some hidden dreams tucked away.

I give you permission right now to be bold and big with your daydreams. No limits. Write what you want, and write what gives you all the feels inside.

> *If we want to live bold, whole, and holy lives,*
> *we have to trust that our hopes and desires*
> *will soften the edges of our sacrifices.*

Something to think about while you make your list. Dig where those dreams are rooted. For example, as I mentioned already, when I was ten I wanted to live in an African bungalow. I don't necessarily want to do that exact thing anymore, but the root of that ten-year-old's dream was planted in my still ever-present desire for adventure and discovering, then living life outside my normal.

Our Father in heaven desires us to dream big so we can enjoy what we do and how we live. He also knows our true desires first come through Him. When we acknowledge these God-given desires and loves from when we were children, a time we were closer to acting on how we are wired, I believe God can stir up these things in us once again.

> Delight yourself in the Lord, and he will give
> you the desires of your heart. (Psalm 37:4)

If you're already living your dreams—then sister, keep on trucking with yo bad self. But if you're not, or if you're living a modified version, it's time to revamp.

Dream big. Plan big.
Go, do, and be big, sister.

## *But, What About . . .*

I can hear it now, because I've already asked myself this question—in many forms.

> What about all the other things?
> What about the money it may take to open a small business or
>    to travel?
> What about the time away from my kids to take a painting
>    class?
> What about needs I have to meet for my family and job?

I hear you. Loud and clear. I'm the biggest dream-big naysayer when it comes to my own dreams. I have an excuse and, sometimes, a legit reason that bumps up against any big and audacious dream I dare to imagine.

But if we want to live bold, whole, and holy lives, we have to trust that our hopes and desires will soften the edges of our sacrifices.

One day during a lunch-break walk, my coworker and friend Kelly and I were laughing about some shenanigans I had shared on my blog the week prior. I was retelling the story to her when she said, "You should write a book."

I laughed because the idea was ludicrous.

Or maybe I laughed in defense. Laughing has always been a type of defense mechanism for me and was here, as well, because her statement struck a lingering chord inside me.

As I was growing up, I filled my journals and notebooks with handwritten stories I'd imagined. I loved reading and writing and loved how words, when pulled together correctly, could create entire new worlds, new ideas, and new realities.

But *real* writers wrote books. So I pitched out all the reasons why that was the dumbest idea ever.

That would take time, which I didn't have with a kid and a full-time job. I wasn't an English major, so I didn't know how to properly string words together with the commas and apostrophes in the correct places. I'd have to find a babysitter or some sort of childcare to take time away to write.

Her response?

"So what? I think you should do it anyway."

*So what?*

A simple question, but it packed a punch. I guess I've never been much of a defensive player. Kelly's words somehow lightened the weight of the sacrifice I knew writing a book would cost.

I think that's what I was afraid of: the cost.

But *so what?*

They were the same words that made training for and running my first half marathon not so big a deal.

Asking "So what?" lightens the weight of sacrifice.

With faith that Christ is able to compensate for our deficiencies, I know this to be true. These words made the burden of what I needed to sacrifice seem just a little less heavy.

So I ask you now,

so what if your dreams will take time to achieve?
so what if it costs money up front?
so what if you're scared?
so what if you don't know the details of where to start?

Christ is able to fill in the answer this "so what" asks of us. He knows the details we don't, and when we take a step of faith toward that thing He's laid on our heart, I believe He'll part the way for us to get there.

Anything worth dreaming is worth paying for and stepping toward.

## The Cost

I recently watched Annie F. Downs do a minisermon via her Instagram stories. She shared a truth from Romans 5 I think we can easily apply here.

> Therefore, since we have been justified by faith, we have peace with God through our Lord Jesus Christ. Through him we have also obtained access by faith into this grace in which we stand, and we rejoice in hope of the glory of God. Not only that, but we rejoice in our sufferings, knowing that **suffering produces endurance, and endurance produces character, and character produces hope**, and hope does not put us to shame, because God's love has been poured into our hearts through the Holy Spirit who has been given to us. (Romans 5:1-5, emphasis mine)

Look at that bolded line, the one that strings together suffering and hope. Suffering to endurance. Endurance to character. Character to hope.

Hope is the end result. When we go through suffering, we have the opportunity to preserve and build character that leads to hope in God's unfailing presence and love.

Yes, this verse is referencing some of the big and heavy things of life. But I think we can apply it here, too, with our personal desires and passions. The basic truth is that hope costs something—but yields something greater.

Hope requires sacrifice.

If we *hope* to start a new Etsy shop with our beloved hobby of hand lettering or making jewelry, it's going to take some sacrifice.

If we *hope* to run a marathon, it's going to take some sacrifice.

If we *hope* to finally plant that garden, it's going to take some sacrifice.

No, we can't always have our cake and eat it too. We can't always spend the evening with our kids if the only classes for that degree we have been craving are at night. We must sacrifice.

This doesn't mean time with kids or our spouses can't be made up. Maybe not in quantity, but definitely in quality.

But we can *hope* to fulfill personal desires and not be disappointed in them, because God created us each uniquely to do and be and love certain things.

One thing I'd like to point out if you'll go back to Psalm 1 with me. (Remember our thriving tree?) Verse 3 says, "He is like a tree planted by streams of water that yields its fruit *in its season*" (emphasis mine).

The reality is we must practice wise discernment when deciding our season to do these things.

If you have a newborn, it may not be your season to travel the world.

If you recently accepted a new job, it may not be your season to take an extended vacation and hike the Grand Canyon.

If your teen children are struggling through a tough semester at school, it may not be your season to indulge in a new side hustle that distracts you from home life for a while.

You know your family's and your limits—for this season.

But just because it may not be your season now to do something doesn't mean that your season won't come later, even soon.

Regardless of when we decide to chase our dreams into our reality, it's going to take sacrifice. And sacrifice, with patient endurance, leads to hope.

## Reverse the Rigor Mortis

It was never a dream of mine to be a long-distance runner. Never.

But it *was* a dream of mine to do something I never thought I could do.

As I ran (jogged? limped?) around a final corner of the downtown Atlanta streets, which were lined with people cheering on the full and half marathoners, I never felt more alive.

Tired, yes. Sore, yes. But alive, for sure.

It's almost like a current of electricity zoomed through my body and mind. (Science-y people might call this adrenaline.)

My pace picked up and my stride lengthened as I crossed the finish line.

And then my legs fell off.

OK, not really, but it sure felt like they did.

It wasn't the 13.1 miles behind me that made me feel alive. Those had nearly killed me.

It was the confirmation in front of me that I had the ability to do something hard and something big that jolted my spirit awake.

That first half marathon of mine happened nine months after I had my first child. I was working full time, nursing a new baby, and supporting my husband's budding business, and I trained for my first long-distance footrace.

I was pretty proud of myself. I still am, actually. Because it was a sacrifice. I took time away from my colicky baby, work, and husband to focus on something I wanted to do. I stole precious hours of sleep from myself that first year of motherhood to go run. I gave up time chatting and eating with friends in order to run during lunch hours.

> *The things that make your heart come alive will be the things that carry you to what you long to accomplish.*

I gave up physically, emotionally, and mentally to run that stupid race that made my legs go into rigor mortis for days.

But wouldn't you know, while my body stiffened and felt the results of the race, my spirit soared and felt the effects of my efforts. The same happened for my spirit as I took on writing this book.

I trained for a half marathon and wrote because of what the end product—the finished race and the completed manuscript—gave me.

What left me feeling alive was the sacrifice itself, not the product.

My sacrifices didn't take away from the experience of running that race or writing a book, they added more to the experience.

It cost something for me to do these things, so they are much more valuable to me than if I had not—quite literally—paid something for them.

I joked about my legs suffering from rigor mortis during the days following my first race, but I think that, more often than not, we may allow a small form of rigor mortis to stiffen our spirits.

Do you know what rigor mortis is? A rather gruesome term, in my opinion. A stiffening of the body's muscles after death, rigor mortis is caused by a depletion of ATP (which stands for a type of chemical compound I absolutely will never be able to pronounce) in body tissues resulting in an unavailability of energy to interrupt contraction of muscle fibers.

In layman's terms, it means there's no substance in there allowing the body to move after death.

What substance are we missing that would allow us to move in the direction of our dreams and desires?

Is it support from family and friends? Ideas on where to get started?

Whatever it is, if we are going to not just stay but come alive, we have got to get moving. We have got to reverse the onset of spiritual or emotional rigor mortis and put some focus back into what we want to do.

The things that make your heart come alive will be the things that carry you to what you long to accomplish.

When our wants, desires, and passions are being met head-on, or at least are on the road to being met, I truly believe our minds and hearts are in a better place to live out a whole and holy life.

Because this is what Jesus had in mind for us.

Each of us was *created* with specific interests, passions, and talents.

Maybe when I ask what makes you come alive, you already know.

Maybe it's been sitting there, just waiting for you to take notice of it and then do something about it. Or maybe you're already walking toward that thing.

But maybe you're like me, and somewhere along the path of birthing children, raising a family, and managing life, you lost hold of what tips you over the edge of surviving to thriving.

There are two easy questions that we can ask to get us brewing on the idea.

What interests you? What are you good at?

The answer to what makes you come alive may not be found in both questions. Maybe the answer is from one or the other. Or maybe it's out in left field, and you only come across it by accident when thinking through the want-to-do list you made a few pages ago.

But these two questions will give you a pretty wide scope of where you may thrive.

If Hugh Jackman were sitting here singing to you and he sang "'Cause you're dreaming with your eyes wide open," what would flash across your mind? Where are you dreaming with your eyes wide open? What are you surrounded by? What are you doing and feeling?

We know we're there—we're *alive*—when we can't fathom going back to the world we were living in.

# More for Mom

PART 3

CHAPTER 8

## More Time

## Prioritizing Minutes in Your
## Relationship with God

On April 8, 2012, Kimberly "Sweet Brown" Wilkins was inter-
viewed on Oklahoma City NBC affiliate KFOR-TV after a fire
rampaged through her apartment complex.

The forty-two-second interview quickly went viral when
Wilkins's hilarious "ain't nobody got time for that" take on the bronchitis she contracted hit the airwaves.

Because TRUTH.

Kimberly Wilkins was absolutely right: nobody has time for
bronchitis, or any other illness for that matter. (And you probably
don't have time to YouTube her video right now, but I'm going to
suggest you do. Enjoy.)

This quote became popular, not just because of her hysterical
delivery but also because of its accuracy and applicability to a whole
range of situations.

Wilkins's point rings true. We don't have time for a lot of
last-minute changes to our regular schedules. We don't have time for

us (or the kids!) to get sick or for the car to break down. We don't have time for traffic jams or slow people in front of us at the grocery store. And we definitely don't have time for "one more thing" on our already full plates.

As a busy working mama, when I hear the word *more* in relation to my everyday, immediate panic ensues and—sometimes—I raise defenses. I scan for ways to guard against adding more to my plate. I make excuses, blame someone or something else, or even pretend there isn't an issue and ignore whatever is trying to wedge itself into my schedule.

However, if we're going to live a whole and holy life, we need to change our mind-set right now and release our hold and preconceived notions on the word *more*.

The word *more* doesn't have to be a burden. If we make the time and space for *more* of the right things, we can begin to live this fully whole and holy life.

## *Do As I Say, Not As I Do*

So let's start with our reality and what we actually do.

Actions speak louder than words. We tell our people, "Do as I say." But if we say our kids, friends, or God are most important in our lives, yet we allow scrolling social media or even the latest episode of *This Is Us* to push aside the time it takes for these relationships, we are not setting the ideal example.

Does this ever happen to you? Because it does to me. I'm just as guilty as the next mama of saying one thing and doing another. Sometimes, the choices we make are not a huge deal, but other times they are large and heavy, and our relationships suffer the consequence.

One morning this past spring, after I flew home from a weekend work trip, I stood in my kitchen over the stove cooking breakfast and scrolling my email inbox. I was trying to decipher which emails I could delete or reply to quickly in order to clear up some space later in my work day.

Meda, my then four-year-old, stood at my feet in her pajamas, tugging at my shirt. I'd like to say I stopped what I was doing to squat down and see what she needed. Instead, I told her that mommy was busy and told her to hurry and go change into school clothes.

This didn't seem like a big deal to me at the time. Surely my email filtering was more important than whatever Meda wanted from me. Because, let's be real, it's normally a question regarding cartoon options or if she can have ice cream for breakfast.

However, it's these tiny, daily examples of not keeping my interactions paramount that accumulate to a sum of misaligned priorities.

Want to know what Meda needed that morning?

"Mommy, I wanted to give you a good morning hug and say I love you. Welcome home."

Her sweet words cut straight to my core.

How sweet is that? And I didn't have time for her loving gesture because I was scrolling junk mail. #MomoftheYear.

Meda quickly snapped me out of my focus on distracting details and into a holy hug.

That's what some of these time suckers are—unnecessary junk. Our priority needs to be the things that bring us closer to holiness; we can let the junk fall to the side.

They are the things that set us apart from every other working mom. From every other stay-at-home mom. And—quite frankly— most everyone else. Because they are things that make Jesus smile since He knows we've aligned our priorities right.

We talked about slipping relationships with others in chapter 4, but what if we do this very same thing—allow others to slip away—not just with the people in our lives, but the God of our lives?

Remember the friendship truth bomb dropped in chapter 4: to have a friend, you have to be a friend, and to have relationship, you have to give relationship? What if we reworked that thought into a holy truth?

To have more Jesus, you have to give more to Jesus.

We know God is always with us, but that doesn't always mean we're with Him.

> Be strong and courageous. Do not fear or be in
> dread of them, for it is the LORD your God who
> goes with you. He will not leave you or forsake
> you. (Deuteronomy 31:6)

The thing Jesus wants most from us is *us*. You and me.

Remember the greatest commandment? This is key when we give ourselves.

> And he said to him, "You shall love the LORD
> your God with all your heart and with all your
> soul and with all your mind. This is the great and
> first commandment." (Matthew 22:37-38)

When we love someone with all our heart, soul, and mind, we make time for that person. We think more about that person, we care more about that person, and more of our entire being is wrapped up in that person.

How do we do this? In order to build a deeper relationship with God and live out our whole and holy lives to the fullest, we must make time for Him.

The problem is that there is a set amount of hours and minutes in our day. We can't add to them, but we can definitely suck some away. So the question I raise is not *if* we have the time, but *where* is the time?

> *We must take care of ourselves physically in order to have the energy to do all the things required of us each day. If we don't have the energy to do all of our tasks, we definitely will not have the energy for Jesus.*

While we mamas are often master time managers, there may be some places where we can streamline our schedule or task list in order to open up more time for Jesus and our priority time with Him.

Let's take a few minutes to self-evaluate and look for ourselves at where our time and energy is currently going and where we can tweak our daily routine to build more margin in for God.

## There's Never Any Time!

Do you remember Jessie Spano from *Saved by the Bell*? My childhood was shaped by the lessons learned at Bayside High in the 1990s with Zack, A. C., Kelly, Screech, and the rest of the gang. Kelly was basically my BFF (I mean, we were both cheerleaders after all) and Zach was just *waiting* for the day I strolled across his path so he could profess his unending love for me.

In one of my favorite episodes, Jessie and the other girls are part of a singing group, and Jessie ends up having a complete breakdown due to the stress (and drugs) she was juggling. If you are a child of the 1980s and 1990s, you absolutely remember this moment.

Jessie sputtered, "There's never any time!" on Zack's shoulder as she dropped, one by one, the caffeine pills from her hand.

Jessie wasn't just out of time, she was out of energy.

I would argue most of us can relate to this level of exhaustion.

It's not that we don't have time, it's that we don't have energy.

Why do you think caffeine pills were Jessie's go-to? Why are any caffeine products our go-to?

I'm a self-proclaimed Starbucks addict, so there's no hating on coffee coming from me. However, I can't deny the point is true. I drink coffee in the morning to help me wake up, to give me energy, and to *keep* me that way.

So where are you on the energy level right now? Are you exhausted? Worn down? Hungry? Shaky? Tired of thinking? Or energized, by chance?

Take a minute and think about it—from head to toe.

We must take care of ourselves physically in order to have the energy to do all the things required of us each day. If we don't have the energy to do all of our tasks, we definitely will not have the energy for Jesus.

Everyone who has ever fallen asleep while praying give a mighty "Amen!" I'm only kidding. I've never fallen asleep while praying. (Yes, I have.)

## Sleep Patterns

> And rising *very early in the morning*, while it was
> still dark, he departed and went out to a desolate
> place, and there he prayed.
>> (Mark 1:35, emphasis mine)

This is where I need to give my fellow non-morning peeps a shout-out, because this part of prioritizing our time with Jesus is not so cool. Well, at least it doesn't always feel as cool as our comfy pillow.

But the truth is, sleep often is what steals our time away from God. Hear me when I say, I am *not* telling you to deprive yourself of sleep, but if there are any other snooze-button lovers out there like me, you know the conviction I'm talking about.

It is as simple as preferring the snooze button over the Bible. (Ouch.)

Just as our walk of faith is going to be a gradual one, lasting our whole lives, we don't have to rush our habit changes either. Waking up an hour or two earlier than normal the first day is likely to back-fire with more exhaustion.

If you're used to waking up at 7:00 a.m., try setting your alarm for 6:45 a.m. instead. Start even smaller and go for 6:55 a.m. that first day, then build up from there to the amount of time you need for Jesus slowly over a few weeks.

Set yourself up to succeed. Set a hard bedtime for yourself, and have your family chip in to help with nightly duties before bed in order to meet that bedtime.

> *Smart devices are not just capable of sucking our time away from God but also capable of facilitating more time with God.*

Or maybe you're the opposite of me. Maybe you need more time in the evening instead of in the morning to devote to priority time with Jesus, when you work the late shift or are caring for a new-born or any number of things that take your mornings.

Jesus graciously sets the example for us.

> In these days he went out to the mountain to
> pray, and *all night he continued in prayer* to God.
> (Luke 6:12, emphasis mine)

147

Yes, there are plenty of times Jesus led by example for morning quiet time, but that doesn't mean He isn't into spending time with you at night. So if this is you, adjust your bedtime later by five, ten, or fifteen minutes slowly over the course of days or weeks in order to get your body used to staying up later.

With either the morning or evening sleep adjustments, make sure the other side of the pillow is adjusted similarly. Go to bed at a decent time to make sure you can get up the next morning, and don't expect to be able to get up earlier than normal when you were up later than usual.

## Time with Jesus on the Run

So much of the modern mama's day is spent on the run. I feel like I live in my car and am always rushing from one place to the next. So we need to look at where we cannot just squeeze in time for Jesus but invite Him along with us between the scheduled spaces of our daily calendars.

I'm going to skip straight to my number one tip for productivity on the run for the sake of time. Use your phone.

Smartphones are quite the invention, aren't they? For so many of us, smartphones and devices can suck a lot of our time needlessly from other things that are more important, but they can also help us manage our time well. Think about what all smartphones have done for us over the last decade.

They've streamlined almost everything we do, see, and touch these days. We can check email while in line at the bank, pay our bills while cooking dinner, schedule PTA meetings while in board meetings, and listen to the news reports while walking to lunch. We can track our children's growth and health records. We even use them to manage and maintain our social lives. I'm looking at you, Facebook.

Smart devices are capable not just of sucking our time away from God (thank you to my daily morning Instagram scroll) but also of facilitating more time with God.

There are plenty of apps that offer devotionals, prayer prompts, daily Scripture notifications, even the actual Bible. A quick app store search will render a huge list for you. Some of my favorites include First 5, YouVersion Bible, Dwell, and IF:Gathering. Some churches, like my own, even have apps with their latest sermon on them.

These apps don't need to take the place of your actual Bible or Bible study and quiet time, but they can definitely be used to enhance and add more minutes to the time you focus on Jesus while out and about in your day. Take Jesus along with you for the daily ride. He's provided phones for us to do just that.

## It's in Your Head

Along with giving ourselves physical energy, space, and time, have you heard of this "mental load" phenomena storming the mommy blog world?

It's the idea that mothers carry the extra burden of handling not just the tangible duties of the household, work, and parenting but also all of the invisible duties. The things we think about all day long: the mental checklists, the appointments we know are on our calendar, the recipes and grocery lists not written down yet, the gift-buying to be done, the time each kid needs to be picked up and dropped off at practice. It's the caring and knowing about everything.

I absolutely believe this mental load to be a thing. A *real* thing. A real, *heavy* thing.

To be completely honest, I don't have a ton of heavy physical tasks on my daily or weekly list that suck my time and energy. I don't work in a setting where I perform manual labor often. I'm also blessed in that my husband is the one who handles most of the yard work, empties the dishwasher, and helps put away the laundered clothes, among other things around the house. I'm a pretty lucky gal.

However, the invisible parts of my job are extremely draining, often leaving me bone tired at the end of each day. I may not be building things by hand or walking miles from patient to patient through hospital hallways, but I have what feels like everything else weighing me down mentally. And this is not just from my paying job.

At home, I'm the one who knows what time practices start and end, which food items in the pantry are running low, and when it's best to leave the house in order not to hit traffic. I'm also the one who makes plans I won't be a part of, who prepacks lunches while considering not only my own daughters' needs but also the list of items containing allergens that could affect their classmates.

I have a terrible memory and am very easily distracted. I believe this is partly because of the changes that child rearing caused in my body and mind, but I also know it's because there are roughly twelve bazillion things running through my mind at any given time.

Maybe this is you too. Or you're the one who is on her feet all day working. Or maybe you're both.

Whether it's racing and distracted minds or aching muscles and sleepy eyes, all of these loads wear us down. Leaving less energy— and therefore time—for the One who can re-energize us.

Friend, can I remind you of something Jesus said?

> Come to me, all who labor and are heavy laden,
> and I will give you rest. Take my yoke upon you,
> and learn from me, for I am gentle and lowly in
> heart, and you will find rest for your souls. For
> my yoke is easy, and my burden is light.
> (Matthew 11:28-20)

When we come to Jesus, tired and burdened, we bring all of that weight with us. He can take it. And this isn't just fluffy, feel-good stuff. He really can.

Let's try it.

## *Dump on Jesus*

Since I can't make you physically rework your capacity levels through the pages of a book, we're going to mentally create room for Jesus together right now. I'm going to trust that you create some physical space and energy on your own.

We're going to take two minutes and do what I call a brain dump. Grab a sheet of paper and write down everything you're thinking about today as bullet points. Use only a few words for each, just enough to jog your memory. The list can be as short or as long as needed. But don't push it—only write down things as they jump into your mind.

For example, here is my brain dump right now:

- Meda's birthday party/gift?
- Podcast recording Thursday
- Staff meeting
- Staff outing next week
- Cycling wives dinner is Friday
- Contract
- Kindergarten registration/shot record
- Blog post for MMB
- McKenna's diagram
- Paint colors for bedroom
- Bryant's race in Nashville
- Wendy's wedding—gift?

- Doctor appointment—Wednesday
- Social media scheduled posts
- Marketing/launch schedule
- New package from Amazon arriving

These are the things currently taking up time and space in my mind, even as I write to you.

> *Do what works best, or do what merely works.*
> *Jesus will work out the rest.*

So go ahead, take a minute to quickly write down everything that crosses your mind. I'll wait right here.

Got it? Next, we're going to dump this list over to Jesus.

Start with this prompt and then go through each line of your brain dump.

> Jesus, you have asked me to come to You with what labors and burdens me, and when I do that, You have promised rest. Your yoke is easy and Your burden light, so right now I lift up [*insert your concerns here*] to You. Take over these things I'm thinking of, Jesus, and make them Your burden. Give my racing mind rest and space for You to come in and fill me up. I'm ready and willing for more of You. In Jesus's Name. Amen.

You've written down and prayed over your brain dump list. Now it's gone.

Seem too easy? Maybe it is. But that's what's awesome about Jesus: His burden is light and easy.

Sure, you can think about these things when they come up, but they're not mulling over and over in your brain, and you've brought

Jesus into it, as well. If they start to mentally race again, rewrite your list and pray it again . . . and again and again as needed. He'll be faithful to ease the load. You've given Him the opportunity to jump into another portion of your day, given Him the time and space allowed into your mental load.

Feel free to cross things off as they pass or are taken care of. However, remember *this is not a to-do list* but a place where we tangibly take what's stealing space in our minds and offer it to Jesus. You can cross something off and thank Jesus for taking care of it or getting you through it.

My friend Amy writes down her brain dump at the start of every morning on a pretty sheet of paper. I'm the one who jots it down on the back of a receipt in my car while at a stoplight. This idea of brain dumping over to Jesus doesn't have to be structured, but it does need to be done.

Do what works best, or do what merely works. Jesus will work out the rest.

## Hem Me In

Jessica Turner wrote *The Fringe Hours* in order to help women practice self-care and do the things they love. She coined the term "fringe hours," which she describes as the pockets of time in our day left unattended. Her book helps women find the time in their already busy schedules to make time for themselves.

I love this concept, love the book, and love her message. However even with a good amount of self-care, sometimes when I'm using my fringe time, I still feel frayed.

Again, I'm a word nerd, so when I was thinking about my fringe time, I looked up the definition of *fringe* so I could really grasp what this time meant to me on a deeper level. It turns out that a fringe is an ornamental way of edging material with threads left loose or formed into tassels.

I have never denied my tendency to overanalyze things. When I'm thinking of my unattended time, I don't normally consider it ornamental and decorative. I like to think that it's important, productive, and effective.

But isn't that how our schedules feel sometimes? Like they are bordered with loose and frayed moments we don't quite know how to best use? Or even moments that are for decorative purposes—to show others what we think they'd appreciate?

Or maybe in the extra minutes here or there, we wonder if we should squeeze in one more load of laundry or another email. Or maybe we wonder if we should use it to read or paint or do some other activity that we enjoy.

Maybe it's the perfectionist in me—or at least the little bit of her that's left after birthing these three rambunctious kids jumping around in the other room right now—but I'd rather know that my time is hemmed and tailored to fit, rather than frayed and ultimately unsuitable for the life God has called me to live.

> You hem me in, behind and before, and lay your
> hand upon me. (Psalm 139:5)

When you hem a piece of cloth, you turn the edge under and sew it. The edge is sewn closed so it doesn't fray.

King David, when writing Psalm 139, understood that God is the one who knows us well enough to keep us hemmed in.

So this is where we allow Him to hem in our fringe time.

Where do our fringe hours go? Do they go to scrolling your phone? Listening to the latest podcast or romance audiobook?

These things are not bad. I even encourage them. However, if they take up all of our free minutes throughout the day, we haven't made space for Him yet and there is little opportunity for Jesus to jump into the daily grind.

What about some of these places? Where else do you find yourself filling the seconds with nothingness rather than godliness?

> In line at the grocery store, in the car line, at the post office, or in the public restroom?
> On the subway, on the bus, or in the carpool?
> At the bus stop waiting for the kids to get home?
> At a stoplight?
> On the elevator?
> Outside the boardroom?
> At work booting up a slow computer?
> In the kitchen waiting for coffee to brew?

Take some of these moments and hem them in with Jesus. Sing a worship song at the stoplight and pray for the people surrounding you on the elevator. Pray for your kids and their classmates on the school bus as it drives to your stop. Write and rewrite a scripture verse on a sticky note as your computer loads.

There is time in the middle of life for Jesus. We just need to maximize our frayed minutes.

## Embrace the Not-So-Quiet Time

When I first became a Christian, people told me I needed to set aside what they called a "quiet time" or "priority time." It was a time of day, whether five minutes or sixty minutes, when I should sit quietly before God, praying, reading the Bible, and worshipping Him.

This picture in my mind comes in the early morning, with my steaming cup of coffee, birds chirping outside my window, me cuddled in a blanket with my Bible open, and Jesus almost tangibly there with me.

> But when you pray, go into your room, close the
> door and pray to your Father, who is unseen.
> Then your Father, who sees what is done in
> secret, will reward you. (Matthew 6:6 NIV)

Everything about Matthew 6:6 makes me want to type in all the praise-hand emoji. Because *quiet, alone, unseen, rewards, secret*—all these words tug at my busy-mom-of-three emotions.

Then reality hits.

Mark 1:35-37 is more my reality.

> Very early in the morning, while it was still dark,
> Jesus got up, left the house and went off to a
> solitary place, where he prayed. Simon and his
> companions went to look for him, and when
> they found him, they exclaimed: "Everyone is
> looking for you!" (NIV)

"Everyone is looking for you!"

Is this your life too? I assume I'm not the only one who gets up and goes to a solitary place to pray, only to be quickly followed by little people, a hungry husband, or needy pets.

Even if I wake earlier than usual, odds are one of the kids will wake up and interrupt this quiet time. Someone will need breakfast or help going potty or help finding a favorite shirt. That's how it is. This is my season of motherhood—a season where my people need me.

So yes, if you are like me, there tends to be very little time to yourself right now.

However, you don't have to be in the Season of Littles to have interruptions and a lack of privacy and silence. Maybe your kids are able to feed and clothe themselves or are even out of the house. So maybe work is the theft of your focus and "quiet" time. With a job constantly bombarding you with tasks, it's hard to pay attention to Jesus when the phone is near and pinging all day long. Or maybe it's a number of other things.

I used to think because of my lack of privacy and silence that my quiet time wasn't meaningful or productive. I'd grow frustrated and even resentful for not getting "ideal" time with God.

This ultimately caused the opposite of the effect I desired. I wanted more time alone with God, to hear from God, and to be close to God. But my frustration and resentfulness toward the very things (the noise, the people) God put "in my way" during my quiet time created a mind-set where I couldn't receive any of His presence, let alone more of it.

I've learned—am learning—that God can and will use my not-so-quiet moments to grow my knowledge and relationship with Him.

Let's be real: most of my life is not so quiet. However, Jesus wants to be involved in all of my life.

I know God is with me wherever I am, whatever I'm doing, and no matter who is around me.

While I still crave and love the actual silence I (sometimes) get with Jesus, I'm learning to roll with it and recognize that not every moment with God has to be perfect and serene. Because REAL LIFE, my friend. There are ways we can intentionally honor our not-so-quiet quiet time with Jesus.

## Keep Him Handy

Keep Scripture quotes, Bibles, devotionals, and prayer prompts handy for when you find a few silent moments throughout the day.

If His Word is right there, it's easy to take advantage of the time that does pop up. This is number one for me. If you walk through my house, you'll see verses posted, a Bible or devotional in different rooms, or a passage from Scripture on my phone screen.

I keep my phone close by me almost all day long (I know, I have a problem), so I can use it while I'm out and about, away from my Bible at home. Playing worship music throughout the morning while getting ready for work or packing lunches can also keep my mind in a worshipful state.

## Plan Ahead

OK, we're going to devote time to God, but we don't know how it's going to turn out, if we'll be interrupted or sidetracked, right?

Pick a Bible-reading plan to follow or a book that studies the Bible. When I wake up, I know which book I'm going to grab and get through what I can. If I have to stop in the middle, I have to stop in the middle. I don't waste time flipping through the Bible, wondering, *Where should I start?*

## Plan Not to Follow the Plan

Let's be real. It isn't always going to play out how we imagine it. So if you are currently trying to read through a Bible study book and you've been unable to sit down to read it, you're going to have to engage a new tactic for the day. Sometimes, I will go back to a Bible reading app or something similar, where there is a ready-made and short devotional quickly available.

Another strategy I use as a backup plan I adapted from the website of my good friend and pastor, Jessica H. Morris.[1]

> [re]**THINK.** Reflect on what you learned or read in
> your last quiet time. Re-ask yourself some questions

about the subject. Ask what stands out most to you about it. What applies to you most personally?

A good strategy here is memorizing Scripture. Take a Scripture verse and meditate on it all day, write it down in an email to yourself, chant it over and over, write it on sticky notes and post them all over your house, or do whatever you need to do to keep thinking about God's Word.

> *People should be inclusions, not interruptions.*
> *Jesus reminds us this is why He and*
> *we are here.*

Here, the goal is to re-engage your brain to meditate on Scripture or what God is telling you. Pay attention to discover if what you're learning is different today than during your last quiet time. Chances are it very well could be.

> [re]PRAY. Pray a prayer familiar to you. Maybe you re-pray what you prayed about yesterday because it's still relevant. Or you pray the Lord's Prayer. Maybe you speak to God through a psalm of thanksgiving (Psalm 100 is a good one) or Psalm 23, both effective and familiar to many.

The goal is simply to speak to God. Speak to Him while you drive, while you shower, while you climb each stair in your home. But to simplify it and be persistent, pray what you've heard or prayed before.

> Be persistent in prayer, and keep alert as you pray,
> giving thanks to God. (Colossians 4:2 GNT)

## Do It Out Loud

OK, so you've woken up early, settled in for some QT with Jesus, and your little one (or husband!) sneaks downstairs and interrupts.

This is often an "UGH" moment for me. But I have to force myself to remember it doesn't have to be, nor does it for you.

We can pull a child up next to us and read out loud, pray out loud, or explain what God is teaching us. Remember in Mark 1:35-37 when Simon exclaimed to Jesus during His quiet time, "Everyone is looking for you"?

Well, do you also remember how Jesus responded?

> "Let us go somewhere else—to the nearby
> villages—*so I can preach there also. That is why I
> have come.*" So he traveled throughout Galilee,
> preaching in their synagogues and driving out
> demons. (Mark 1:38-39, emphasis mine)

He taught.

Let's take a page out of Jesus's book, and when people are looking for us, let's teach them and pray for and with them.

People should be inclusions, not interruptions. Jesus reminds us this is why He and we are here.

While I've taken an entire chapter to discuss realigning our time and energy back toward Jesus, in actuality, none of this should take a lot of effort. Simple and small adjustments to our sleep patterns, minutes spent moving throughout our schedule, and even prepping for adjustments to our quiet or priority time will allow more of God to slip into our day.

If we don't do these things, we'll continue to allow our time to slip away from God.

> The heart of man plans his way, but the LORD
> establishes his steps. (Proverbs 16:9)

A day without time for God?

In the grand scheme of things, we're the ones who "ain't got time for that" because He is the Creator of our time and of our days. I think Kimberly "Sweet Brown" Wilkins would agree.

## Note

1. Jessica H. Morris, "[Re]sources," jessicahmorris.com/resources/.

# CHAPTER 9

# More Fasting

## Eliminating What Isn't Drawing You Closer to God

I stood in the middle of my living room over a stray shoe, blood pressure rising. My phone buzzed with urgent texts from my boss and coworker while dirty plates glared at me from the table and my two youngest screamed over a doll. I could hear the dog drinking out of the toilet in the other room, splashing who-knows-what everywhere.

I didn't know what exactly was wrong. I should be used to shoes in the middle of the floor, dirty dishes, arguing kids, and desperate texts from coworkers. This was normal. Even the dog being gross was normal. So why was it all irking me this time? Why was I extra grumpy?

"Mom, go eat. You're hangry."

My daughter McKenna spoke with authority from her after-school station on the couch. Her eyes swept over me before casually looking back to *Fuller House* on Netflix. We had barely walked in the door from work and school, and it was clear, even to an eight-year-old, that I needed to eat.

I'm embarrassed that my daughter had to remind me what I needed. I was hungry. And that made me angry.

I was "hangry."

I hadn't eaten since breakfast or lunch and was feeling the physical and emotional effects late in the afternoon. I'm sure you've had that same feeling before. My body lacked the nourishment needed to function.

> *There is power in stripping away what holds us back from experiencing Him. When we're too busy to pay attention, there's a richness we lose by trying to feed our souls with anything but Him.*

I nodded and turned back to the kitchen. I needed food before diving into the fiasco of my everyday life. Even if that meant eating kids' cheese sticks or Uncrustables sandwiches.

Confession: I don't have the best dietary habits because of my lack of skills and desire to be in the kitchen. I dislike cooking and tend to only eat what is readily available. It's silly, I know, but I just don't like the time or effort it takes to prepare food.

As I was thinking about this in my hangry stupor, it hit me that my relationship with the kitchen is sometimes like my relationship with God. I get lazy and distracted.

Ouch. It's true, though. Is it for you sometimes too?

He's right there, waiting to fill us with good things. It's actually easier than preparing food. All we do is just come to Him—even "hangry." We get to engage, learn from and about Him. It takes trust, faith, and communion, which take time. But it isn't all the prep work we associate with everyday chores. It's truly the most nourishing thing we can do for ourselves.

But we sense that time constraint. We have appointments to keep, work to produce, families to love on, friends to laugh with, and goodness, we have to sleep at some point too!

In the effort to do all these good things (which include roughly one billion small things underneath them), we're left with little time for solitude and much time for interruption and distractions from God. But this thing we've got going on with Jesus? It's a relationship. It takes time and effort, which we've already talked about.

But sometimes the effort needs to come in elimination. Sometimes we need to fast.

## *Why Fast?*

I hear of people fasting. They do a juice fast or some other sort of dietary fast to jump-start their metabolism toward a weight loss goal or to cleanse their bodies.

However, spiritual fasting isn't often discussed in the Christian circles I'm a part of, and it may not be discussed (or practiced) on a regular basis in yours either.

Let's be real. It takes effort, planning, and sacrifice. None of this is fun or easy when we have so much going on.

But in our quest to recognize our wholeness and holiness in Christ and believe Him for more on this side of heaven, fasting should become a regular practice for us. Why? Because there is power in stripping away what holds us back from experiencing Him. Our busyness often leads us to miss out on the holiness He brings. When we're too busy to pay attention, there's a richness we lose by trying to feed our souls with anything but Him.

Fasting was a regular spiritual practice of the Jews and early Christians, and I believe it can accelerate us into a deeper relationship with God, aligning our wholeness and holiness more closely with Christ's. By denying ourselves, fasting reminds us we cannot survive without sustenance. This is true spiritually too. Christ is the "bread of life," and spiritual fasting deepens our desire for this bread (John 6:48), therefore deepening our relationship with God.

I want to start off by saying, if you don't want to fast, don't feel compelled by me to fast. The desire or conviction should come from God, as well as what to fast from, such as food, screen time, online shopping, Starbucks, or even certain topics of conversation. I think you'll know what God wants you to fast from if you'll just ask Him.

Maybe He's saying, "Hey there. This thing that has your attention? It's keeping us from being even closer."

Whatever that thing is, let God speak into your life about it.

If you feel God is not asking you to fast at this point in time, then—*oh my mercy*—don't do it! You should spend time asking what would help enhance your relationship with Him. If it's a physical fast, then you're going to want to seek medical counsel from your doctor before entering any type of food abstinence to make sure it's a good option for you.

What about this discipline is so special? Answering *what* fasting is will give us the *why* we should.

At its most basic level, to fast is to go without food or drink for a period of time. These days, many use it as a jump-start for physical healing and weight loss. Removing toxins and impurities will give our bodies a clean slate to receive what *does* make us more healthy. To fast is to go without having our earthly needs and/or cravings met and nourished.

Fasting shifts focus from physical nourishment (food) to spiritual nourishment (Jesus). Our focus is taken off preparing and taking in food and instead put on preparing our hearts. We are showing God that He has our attention and He is our focus. We desire Him and put aside nourishing our bodies, expecting God to move in our hearts when we place Him above physical needs.

Spiritual fasting is much the same as fasting for physical reasons. It is a complete reset of the mind and body to slingshot us into a more nourished spiritual life.

This can also mean fasting from other cravings or "needs" besides food. It could look like abstinence from screens, spending money on ourselves, or any number of things that take up more attention than God does.

## What Does God Say About Fasting?

Fasting is all over the pages of the Bible, especially in the Old Testament. Moses fasted before receiving the Ten Commandments, Hannah fasted before bearing Samuel, David fasted when his child was ill, Elijah fasted while escaping Jezebel, then a widow fasted for Elijah, and Daniel fasted from the king's delicacies. The list goes on.

Want to know what I love about God? He lays out everything we need to know about what He wants from us in the Bible. Isaiah 58 explains what is true and false fasting.

I would be doing you a disservice if I didn't allow you to read through parts of that chapter right now, so take a minute to hear what God tells us about fasting through Isaiah 58:3-9.

> "Why have we fasted, and you see it not?
>     Why have we humbled ourselves, and
>     you take no knowledge of it?"
> Behold, in the day of your fast you seek your
> own pleasure,
>     and oppress all your workers.
> Behold, you fast only to quarrel and to fight
>     and to hit with a wicked fist.

Fasting like yours this day
   will not make your voice to be heard on high.
Is such the fast that I choose,
   a day for a person to humble himself?
Is it to bow down his head like a reed,
   and to spread sackcloth and ashes under him?
Will you call this a fast,
   and a day acceptable to the LORD?

Is not this the fast that I choose:
   to loose the bonds of wickedness,
   to undo the straps of the yoke,
to let the oppressed go free,
   and to break every yoke?
Is it not to share your bread with the hungry
   and bring the homeless poor into your house;
when you see the naked, to cover him,
   and not to hide yourself from your own flesh?
Then shall your light break forth like the dawn,
   and your healing shall spring up speedily;
your righteousness shall go before you;
   the glory of the LORD shall be your rear guard.
Then you shall call, and the LORD will answer;
   you shall cry, and he will say, "Here I am."
If you take away the yoke from your midst,
   the pointing of the finger, and speaking
   wickedness.

When you can, go read the whole chapter, but for now let's look more closely at a few of these verses.

Verses 5-7 give us the three major reasons to fast:

     1. humble ourselves

     2. free the oppressed

     3. take care of others

A lot more specific requests and detailed reasons can fall under these umbrella motivations, but these are the biggies.

Under Mosaic law, Jews were required to fast at least one day, on the Day of Atonement, humbling themselves before God (Leviticus 23:26-32). But they also fasted in times of great sorrow and in response to great disasters (Psalm 35:13; Judges 20:24-26).

The Jews fasted and wept when they learned of Haman's plans to exterminate them. Queen Esther interceded on their behalf but called them to continue fasting along with her and her maidens (Esther 4:3-16). They participated in this fast in order to take their minds off earthly threats and to pray and praise and glorify God before the queen approached the king about the danger. God saw Esther and the Jews' hearts and saved them.

In 2 Samuel 12, King David fasted when his child became very ill. His elders came and tried to get him to eat, but he remained in the same place fasting until the child's death days later. David was hoping God would see him and be gracious to his longing (v. 21) and cure the child. Even though God didn't answer David's prayers as he wished, David still worshipped the Lord after his child died and grew closer to his God through the process.

These examples show God's people fasting in times of distress, as a means to take care of others and free others from oppression, but it can also be done when we are merely wanting to stay clean and holy, humble ourselves, and not be spoiled by things of this world, much like Daniel did in the Old Testament.

Daniel and his friends did a partial fast, refusing the meat in the king's court where he and his friends were taken to be trained. They continued eating but ate only fruits and vegetables with water. In the end, God blessed them with wisdom for their faithfulness so they stood in favor before the king (Daniel 1:17-21). This fast was in order to cleanse the physical body of food that didn't coincide with God's best plan for them.

The New Testament tells us about fasting by some of the major players. John the Baptist, Paul, and oh, ya know . . . *Jesus*. They all fasted for one of the three reasons listed in Isaiah 58:5-7.

After Saul saw Jesus on the road to Damascus (Acts 9), he was blinded and didn't eat or drink anything for three days. During this time, he humbled himself and gained divine wisdom of his identity in and calling from Christ.

Jesus's fast in the desert was a key point as He started His ministry, where He fulfilled *all* of the reasons to fast found in Isaiah 58.

These are the reasons to fast that God has demonstrated and chosen for us: to humble ourselves, promote freedom, and help others. (See Isaiah 58:5-7.)

If you have time to work your Google magic, you'll find that the fasts mentioned in the Bible are always accompanied with *more* of God—His miracles, His presence, His promises.

It didn't matter if it was a partial, short, long, private, or corporate fast. God showed up in and after every fast. Just as Isaiah 58 promises, He will go with you and heal you (v. 8), answer you (v. 9), guide you (v. 11), and delight you (v. 14).

> *Fasting may be the kick-start you need to take your eyes off the concerns of this world and put them on the One who makes you whole and holy, to make Him more present.*

While God doesn't owe us a miracle or an answer for our fasting, I believe He will reward us with more of Him if our mind-set and heartbeat are laser beamed straight at His character, *because He chooses to.*

He is the reward.

It's important to note that under the new covenant in the New Testament, fasting is not *commanded*, however it is *assumed* that Christ followers will do so. Matthew 6:16-18 says,

> *And when* you fast, do not look gloomy like the hypocrites, for they disfigure their faces that their fasting may be seen by others. Truly, I say to you, they have received their reward. *But when you* fast, anoint your head and wash your face, that your fasting may not be seen by others but by your Father who is in secret. And your Father who sees in secret will reward you. (emphasis mine)

While we are not required to fast, Jesus did say, "and *when* you fast." That sounds like a pretty solid assumption.

If Jesus expects us to and did it Himself, I'm going to say it is something we should consider doing as well.

Fasting can be a good response for us when danger is near, trials await at work, heartaches pop up, or we feel stale in our vigor for Jesus and reading His Word.

The following questions have challenged me, so you may want to ask yourself some as well:

- Have work emails taken over the very first and very last moments of your day?
- Has managing your household distracted you from managing your spiritual life?

- Do you need to focus on God more than work, your daily routine, your kids' after-school activities, or your online presence?
- Do you want to hear Jesus's voice more than your own?
- Would you like to see God move in a part of your life, and are you willing to give up whatever it takes to do so?

When asked about His disciples' fasting habits, Jesus responded, "The attendants of the bridegroom cannot mourn as long as the bridegroom is with them, can they?" (Matthew 9:15 NASB).

> *We live in a culture where luxuries are perceived as necessities, and they don't include just food anymore.*

He goes on to say that once He is gone, they would fast. He views fasting and mourning together, neither of which is necessary when He is present.

For many of us, Jesus isn't as "present" as we could allow Him to be.

Fasting may be the kick-start you need to take your eyes off the concerns of this world and put them on the One who makes you whole and holy, to make Him more present.

More intimate communion with Christ will illuminate the vibrancy of our everyday life. Let's make sure *we* are not the ones becoming the greatest hindrance to our wholeness.

## What Needs Eliminating?

To live a whole and holy life, we need to eliminate whatever causes separation from God and keeps us from the nourishment of

Christ. Sometimes—many times—that's food. We focus on food constantly and indulge in it more than we indulge in God. Food is always a good starting point for regular fasting in your life.

> *Whatever isn't drawing us closer to God is ultimately pulling us away from Him. When we aren't close or constantly getting closer to God, we should fast.*

However, we live in a culture where luxuries are perceived as necessities, and they don't include just food anymore.

Consider the smart devices always in our hands, the television shows recorded on our DVRs, online shopping during lunch break, and Facebook constantly on cue.

Hello, my name is Kristin, and I'm a social media addict. (The first step is admitting you have a problem.)

It's like my thumb knows exactly how many times to swipe and which direction to tap to open that little blue square of Facebook or the tiny radiant one of Instagram. Scrolling the beautiful feeds and adorable baby pictures of my friends' kids (and my own!) fills me up.

Or so I think.

Is looking into the lives of others nourishing and filling me? Where is God in this? Is He there at all? Shouldn't He be more fulfilling than these things?

I have friends who are hardly ever on social media but cannot get off the couch for hours and hours because the latest episodes of *Game of Thrones* and *This Is Us* made it to the queue.

I give my husband a hard time because he falls into what I call the "YouTube Vortex of Doom." You know the one. And it's a deep, dark pit, my friend. Maybe you don't have an issue with television, social media, or technology, but my guess is there is something in your daily, weekly, or monthly routine interfering with your ability to discern between what you *need* and what you *want*.

Maybe it's something simple you indulge in, or maybe it's as serious as an addiction to porn, alcohol, or overspending.

Even if we feel in control of these things, a fast may still be in order because whatever isn't drawing us closer to God is ultimately pulling us away from Him.

When we aren't close or constantly getting closer to God, we should fast.

Our cravings for anything other than God are what our church friends call "worldly" desires. They are driven by the sin of man and they lead to sins.

> *Fasting breaks us out of the world's routines.*
> *And if our motivations are right, we can*
> *redirect our hearts to a holy routine.*

Did you catch that? Sin, *singular*, is a power that leads us to commit sins, *plural*. Our cravings and desires are urging us to fulfill them with things that separate us from God. Sins are what we actively engage in that are not of God.

We need to give Jesus space to transform our worldly desires into holy desires. He can and He will if we eliminate what's taking up that room in us.

My best fast was a recent forty-day break from Facebook. I removed all apps, notifications, and reminders of Facebook from my day-to-day. It was weird at first when my fingers automatically tried to open the missing app. It was so tempting to get on Facebook to check the latest news stories and political rants (this was immediately following President Trump's inauguration) to see what shenanigans were happening.

But after a while it got easier, and then quickly it got better. I was more relaxed with more time to focus on work, prayer, or playing with my kids. God spoke to me during that time and granted me the grace to know Him and the people in my life a little better and deeper.

I remember one particular instance when my sister-in-law and mother-in-law came over for dinner, riled up from a post they read on Facebook earlier that day.

Because I had no idea what the original post said, I asked questions to understand what they were so upset about. Their answers led to more questions and more answers. By the end of the conversation, I had a better understanding of their views and why they reacted the way they did. It turns out their passionate response was rooted in a place of hurt and rejection from their family history. It was something I didn't know or understand before the conversation.

Had I seen the post and the comments on social media, I wouldn't have asked the questions leading into the deep discussion. In fact, I may have had preconceived notions that blocked my ability to empathize or listen well.

Something as simple as not reading a post on Facebook led to a more complex understanding of my loved ones. I believe God used that simple post I never saw to deepen my relationship with them, even if just the tiniest bit.

*The ease and simplicity of our internet culture can deplete us of real nourishment. We can't live wholly or holy by simply filling the cravings the world sets in front of us.*

Who knew removing Facebook could do all that?

Fasting breaks us out of the world's routines. And if our motivations are right, we can redirect our hearts to a holy routine.

Another time, during a three-day food fast, I dropped to my knees and desperately asked God to take away the ache in my stomach. Then I prayed I would always know the ache in my stomach if God was not filling it. As I lay on the floor, Jesus slowly eased my pain, steadied my shakiness, and cleared my head. I was reminded of His promises in Isaiah 58:8-14.

Fasting is the intersection where we turn from what we want and head down the road to what we need.

It's a place of repentance and reconciliation with our Maker, where we call and the Lord answers, "Here I am" (v. 9).

It's the place where thoughts of and discussions with God command the very first and last moments of our days.

It's the place where our spiritual life influences and manages our home life.

It's the place where we hear Jesus's voice more than our own or anybody's around us.

Desperate people won't leave without being fed. With fasting, we use our discipline to focus on receiving nourishment more *from* and *of* God. More of His presence and the deeper things that really matter.

When we fast, we reset ourselves quickly to a more natural and needy place to receive the Bread of Life. When Jesus was in the wilderness alone after fasting for forty days and nights, He reminded us—and Satan—that we are not meant to live on food alone but by God's Word (Matthew 4:4).

## Counterfeit Living

While we're talking about it, let's jump deeper into Jesus's forty-day fast for a bit because there is so much goodness and truth hidden in His wilderness experience.

Right after Jesus was baptized, He was led into the wilderness to be tempted by Satan. While out there, He fasted. Then Satan tried to get Jesus to turn stones into bread.

> And after fasting forty days and forty nights, he was hungry. And the tempter came and said to him, "If you are the Son of God, command these stones to become loaves of bread." (Matthew 4:2-3)

Jesus mic-dropped an answer right back.

> But he answered, "It is written,
> 'Man shall not live by bread alone,
>       but by every word that comes from the
>       mouth of God.'" (Matthew 4:4)

Verse 2 tells us Jesus was hungry. And the tempter said that, just like that, Jesus could turn stones into bread.

Jesus could have easily made those stones into *whatever He wanted*. Whatever He wanted to fill His cravings.

We do this all the time in the sense of our on-demand lifestyles.

We live in a culture of same- and next-day deliveries, on-demand entertainment, even online medical care. It's no wonder we don't feel we have to trust God. It's no wonder we see fewer believers in our day. We can get what we want, usually *when* we want.

We don't feel we have to live on God's Word alone because we have the bread we made from stones.

Whatever it is we are craving, we can so easily get it.

But friend, this is counterfeit living. If we are using these cravings to fill an emptiness only God can, then these cravings are nothing but stones.

Matthew 4:4 tells us those stones are counterfeit bread. The ease and simplicity of our internet culture can deplete us of real nourishment. We can't live wholly or holy by simply filling the cravings the world sets in front of us.

So here again is the question I asked earlier. What's been feeding you recently? Is it stones disguised as bread? In order to answer this, you'll want to consider the prompting in your heart. What do you sense you need to give up in order to access a deeper relationship with Him?

## *Where Do I Start?*

So you've decided to abstain from whatever prevents you from drawing closer to Christ.

There are approximately 789 billion-ish resources and suggestions on fasting available from Google, your library, and the Bible, but I'll give you my three best suggestions on how to get started with a successful fast right here. You're a busy woman, so I'm here to save you time.

### 1. Start Small

If you want to do an extended fast (forty days, for example), start off small with one, two, or three days to make sure your body doesn't retaliate too harshly. Maybe your small start is even skipping a single meal each day for a week, then moving up from there. (Before beginning a dietary fast, you should consult your doctor for medical counsel.)

Working up slowly to longer and more stringent fasts will train our bodies and minds to physically abstain from what we're craving.

Starting small helps me know I will be successful. Let's face it. I don't like doing things I won't do well, so I want to know going in that I'll succeed. So I recommend the same for you.

This step should also be taken when breaking a fast. Especially after an extended fast, your body may reject eating an entire pizza for the first meal. So you'll want to integrate food slowly, and take slow steps here and there instead of a radical shift that you can't keep up.

## 2. Plan Ahead

Decide what you'll fast from and for how long. Set a goal and stick to it, maybe using a calendar, a journal, an app, or some other method to help you.

The number one thing to plan ahead for is temptation. You *will* get hungry. You *will* want to check Facebook. You *will* want to do whatever it is you are giving up. So plan to be tempted.

If possible, plan the timing of your fast. It might be hard to fast during the week of a big benefit dinner your company is hosting or the week of your department's big social media campaign, so plan around those things.

Plan ways to reroute your ordinary to experience the extraordinary benefits of your fast. As mentioned before, when you remove temptation, there is a better chance you'll be successful in your fast, which will ultimately lead to more room for Jesus to show up.

If you are removing something besides food, plan on ways to avoid it. Remove any apps or games from your phone, or drive a different route from work if the Target you normally pass has a gravitational pull on you. Turn off your smartphone and have your number forwarded to a landline so you won't be tempted to use your device.

When you fast from food, you'll need to make sure to plan on drinking plenty of water. Have water bottles stationed at your desk waiting for you or keep a refillable bottle near at all times. Place a bottle in the nursery or in the laundry room if you frequent those rooms most often. Trust me on this, water is a faster's best friend. Broth also helps keep sodium and mineral levels up, helping you to feel OK.

You will also need to make time for prayer, which leads me to my last point.

## 3. Pray!

There's something important to note about the fasts in the Bible we discussed earlier. Remember how I told you God showed up in some way or another for every fast in the Bible? God only showed up because the fasting was accompanied by prayer.

> However, this kind does not go out except by prayer and fasting. (Matthew 17:21 NKJV)

Fasting without prayer is, quite simply, starvation.

It's the prayer aspect of fasting that unleashes God's power in and around us. It's the prayer accompanied by a spiritual, emotional, and physical hunger that feeds us. If you aren't sure what to pray, I recommend starting in Matthew 6, the chapter where Jesus teaches about giving, worry, and anxiety. He also teaches how to pray with the Lord's Prayer (Matthew 6:5-15).

I don't believe it's coincidence that *immediately* following the Lord's Prayer, Jesus told us how to fast.

This assures us that with prayer, according to His will, there will be fasting. It's a natural combination. We need to understand the power of fasting and prayer will be released as long as it's done not to *look* godly and holy but to truly *be* godly and holy (vv. 16-18), and we have truly humbled ourselves.

## Prayer Prompts

Because I believe it's so crucial, I've included a few prayers touching on each of the fasts we discussed earlier. Personalize and modify as needed to fit your situation, your friends/family, and your specific fast.

> Father, your Word says you have chosen fasting as a way for us to humble ourselves. Lord, I often forget I was made from mere dust and begin to think and live in a me-centered mind-set. As I remove this thing You've asked me to fast from, remind me with every craving and temptation that You are the center of my life and I don't need—nor should I want—what the world gives. I submit all my anxieties and cares to You, because You care for me. Forgive me for forgetting to always put You first and allowing daily life to get forefront in my mind and heart. You are the one true sovereign and holy God. Be with me through this fast and constantly remind me of who You are. Thank You, Jesus, for sustaining me. In Jesus's name. Amen.

> Gracious God, You have chosen fasting as a way to loosen the bonds of wickedness and oppression. Jesus, I ask for help in turning my cravings toward You in order to undo the straps of this yoke holding onto me (or my friend/family). You are the God of freedom and can break every chain that binds. Jesus, deliver me/us from this and any influence not of You. Forgive me for allowing myself to become chained. I confess my sin(s) to you now. Undo the straps of the yoke over me. In the name of Jesus, deliver me, Father. Amen.

> Father, thank You for the insight to know I need to fast to help _____. Jesus, help me to use this fast for [him/her] and for others. Remind me I shall not live on bread alone, but on the Word of God. May this sacrifice You're asking of me glorify Your name and

serve Your people so they see You. May this sacrifice
feed the hungry and cover or protect the naked and
homeless. Bless _____ and fill me. Help me to
be filled with the act of serving rather than longing for
what I am giving up. Jesus, may we see, hear, and feel
more of You through this time. Thank You, Father, for
this opportunity. In Jesus's name. Amen.

## Hints for Home

For many of us, our family's meals depend on us, and we have
temptations while we are fasting. Here are just a few of the best hints
for home.

- Meal prep for your family for the week, and make easy meals
  they can reheat or grab themselves.
- Use dinner time as prayer time, and disappear to your bedroom or on a walk during meals to use that time for prayer
  or worship.
- Label water bottles with your name, and tell your family they
  aren't allowed to use them this week.
- Play worship music loudly, and pray in the kitchen if/when
  you are fixing meals for your family.
- Have your provider put a freeze on your cable to avoid certain shows or change your service.
- Write encouraging Bible verses on sticky notes, and leave
  them throughout your house to remind you of Him.

## Wisdom While Working

We can't be fooled into thinking fasting will be easier while
we're at work. In fact, that's where much of our mindless intake of

unhealthy things comes from. So try these few tips during work hours to ease the cravings.

- Tell your coworker you'd rather grab coffee or a smoothie than lunch to chat about the next big event.
- Take a prayer walk outside during lunch.
- Find a different route to your desk that doesn't pass the break room or vending machines.
- Set up an app on your phone to bring up Bible verses during the day that will remind you of your focus.
- Set up blocks on your computer to keep certain social media or websites from distracting you.

## Troubleshooting

As I write this chapter, I'm in the first few days of a fast. I'm in a fast of humbling myself in order to hear from God and share His message.

But some of our habits are so engrained in us, we don't even realize when we slip back into them. Just today, I found myself on autopilot, digging through my coworker's candy drawer for a mini Snickers. Oops. I quickly remembered I was fasting from food as a way to focus on Jesus meeting my needs—not myself meeting my needs. I closed the candy drawer. I almost messed up. But even if I had eaten a Snickers, Jesus would have loved me the same. I could still hear from Him and experience the gifts of fasting and time spent with Him.

But we often lose our focus, and the enemy tries to lure, distract, and tempt us to focus on anything *but* Jesus.

The reality is we mess up, even and *especially* when trying so hard. This is true beyond fasting and in our everyday lives.

Here's my advice if this happens. Forgive it, forget it, and forge through the fast.

Ask God for mercy and keep going. I believe God will see your heart and reward you for your desire to eliminate what is keeping Him from you. Talk to Him and ask for help in maintaining your fast.

Our effort and time in doing this will be rewarded with more of Him. He will give us Himself—the Father, Son, and Holy Spirit. We will hear from Him and understand how He sees us and forgives us.

So let's not be as lazy in our relationship with God as I can be in the kitchen. The reward of being wholly Jesus's girl is too great.

> May we draw closer to God, even when—*especially* when—we dread the effort it takes.
> May we focus on His holiness, especially when craving worldliness.
> May we receive more of God while eliminating what's not of God.

That is a recipe that sounds pretty good to me.

CHAPTER 10

## *More Life*

## Finding the *More* We've Been Looking For

The other day I ran into a friend I hadn't seen in a while. After the big hugs and excited heeeyyys! the bumper question came. *"How's life?"*

Because I've never been one to pass by an opportunity to talk about my family or myself, I dove into the endless abyss of filling her in on "life." I started with the kids, mentioning how Rockie May was absolutely in the middle of a crazy phase and how I was looking for a toddler-aged military boarding school before her next birthday when she'd officially be a "threenager." (I was only sort of joking.)

I reminded her (just in case she hadn't been on Facebook to see my *absolutely adorable* end-of-school photos) how Meda just finished preschool and is pumped to start kindergarten in the fall but is dreading getting her kindergarten vaccines that still sit on our to-do list. Oops.

McKenna just finished third grade (where does the time go??) and has opted to take the summer off from art lessons to try vocal lessons instead. Grammys, here we come! But of course I managed to accidentally schedule these lessons at the worst time of the week due to work, so I needed to figure out how to finagle getting my babysitter to get her there.

Then I leapt into Bryant's latest business endeavors and how his cycling races have been derailed for health reasons.

And so on, and so on.

"So yeah, things are busy—really busy. But good, overall," I stopped to catch my breath.

She smiled, shook her head, and said, "I wouldn't expect anything less from you."

I laughingly blew off her comment with a nonchalant, "Yeah, well . . . you know me."

We continued to catch up and promised each other to meet for coffee sooner rather than later.

As we parted, her comment didn't sit well in my stomach. She said she wouldn't expect anything less. From me.

It was especially bothersome because upon asking her how her life was, she had responded, "It's actually extremely good right now. I stepped back from volunteering at the school and even removed email from my phone so I won't bring work home anymore. So I go to work, come home, and enjoy my family. I only do the things I want to do now, the things that give me and my family pleasure. With zero agenda or to-dos. Even the kids are embracing this whole peaceful season. We've given all of that extra stuff up."

Hold up. Stop. Collaborate and listen.

Let me tell you about Mrs. "We've Given That Up."

This friend is Room Mom of the Universe. Pinterest Party Planner of the Century. She makes good money, providing well financially for her family alongside her husband and the home life she manages.

She is a get-'er-done doer, a multitasking guru, and someone who doesn't just survive but thrives in busyness and chaos. She is that friend about whom I consistently ask, "How does she do it all?"

Because she does. All of it. She works hard, plays hard, and looks fantastic doing it.

But she gave it all up. All the extra details, all the extra busy, all the extra stress and worry—all the extra.

Of course she still has lots of responsibilities and things on her to-do lists—she's a business owner and mom, after all—but it was the mind-set of the day-to-day strive, the detail-focused angst, the things that didn't fill her up that she gave up.

She gave up juggling the pieces for embracing the whole.

## Pieces of the Whole

If I asked you right now, "How's life?" what would your answer be? Would you respond with something like "busy," "hard," "hectic," "full," or "going by so fast"?

My answer always seems to include a few of these words. Sure, there are seasons when life is slower and less chaotic, but even when it is, how often do we resort back to this type of answer?

"Oh, you know, it's life."

"Same ol', same ol'."

> *Life is a big thing. In fact, it's THE thing we've got going on.*

It's funny, if I ever answered differently, I'd probably get some weird looks. Just like I was taken aback by my friend's answer.

"Gosh, life is so slow right now. I don't even know what to do with myself. We are in a complete season of peace and rest, and it's utterly joyful."

I'm laughing, thinking of trying to answer like this. My friends would think I was dying or something. Seriously. They'd call my husband and tell him to take me in to the ER because they KNOW MY LIFE.

Besides, I don't use the word *joyful* in everyday talk, let alone pin *utterly* to the front of it.

But bless it, what I wouldn't give to honestly answer this way.

Even when I don't have a zillion things to do, I still *feel* like I do because there are always a zillion things racing through my mind. Remember that mental load we discussed earlier? That is what's causing me to poorly juggle all the pieces of life.

Maybe it is for you too. Or, maybe, it's the actual physical back and forth of the day-to-day. Maybe it's both.

But life modeled by Jesus meant more than just the day-to-day. He talked of how we live our days as a whole.

I've come to think that we sell ourselves short, often just barely making it across the finish line each day. I jumped into the conversation with my friend with all the details—which, quite frankly, she probably did not even care about—but I was missing the main thing.

Ultimately, she asked how "life" was.

Why aren't we answering these "how's life" questions with the big picture in mind?

Life is a big thing. In fact, it's THE thing we've got going on.

We become so laser-focused on one, two, or even three areas that we're not paying attention to everything else. In micromanaging the planting, growing, and pruning of the trees, we miss the beauty of the forest we've cultivated. We can't see the forest for the trees.

What are these trees for you?

Remember in the first chapter together we talked about how our lives aren't actually compartmentalized? Our human brains segregate our work life, mom life, or social life, and so we get swept up in these segregated details without thinking how these pieces complete the whole of our lives.

These parts and pieces of life equal the one life He planned for us at in the beginning.

Being that we're close to ending our time together, I have to remind you that without Him, we merely give pieces to what could be a complete and abundantly WHOLE life.

So which way do we go from here?

Well, I'm so glad you asked.

## *The Way to More Life*

We work to provide for our families and to enjoy the talents we have. But it's not just about having food we prepare and clothing we wear. These are just an area of small trees we've planted in our forest.

> Then Jesus said to His disciples, "Therefore I tell
> you, do not worry about your life, what you will
> eat, or about your body, what you will wear. For
> life is more than food, and the body more than
> clothes." (Luke 12:22-23 NIV)

Life is more than what we put into it.

Our body is more than what we put over it.

Life is Who we allow to complete it, and our body is Who we allow to fill it.

> Jesus said to him, "I am the way, and the truth,
> and the *life*. No one comes to the Father except
> through me." (John 14:6, emphasis mine)

It's about Him completing us, making us whole. And it's about His godliness sanctifying us, making us holy. As complete beings in Christ, we are holy and set apart for His purposes—the people around us.

It's how we show Him to them—our coworkers, family, friends, and those we meet along the way.

This is His will for you. His will for me.

This is His will for us, summed up in Matthew 28.

> And Jesus came and said to them, "All authority
> in heaven and on earth has been given to me. Go
> therefore and make disciples of all nations, baptiz-
> ing them in the name of the Father and of the Son
> and of the Holy Spirit, *teaching* them to *observe*
> all that I have commanded you. And behold, *I am*
> *with you always*, to the end of the age."
> (Matthew 28:18-20, emphasis mine)

Verse 20 says to "teach" them to "observe."

When we do this, He is with us always—always.

Jesus never described His life the way we often describe our own, as "busy" or "chaotic." Let's take a look at a typical day for Him.

Mark 1:21-33 is a great example of a regular day in the life of Jesus. This day that Jesus and His disciples went into Capernaum was the Sabbath, so He went to the synagogue (like our modern-day church), and got to work helping people. Talking to people, teaching them, and even healing them.

> They went into Capernaum; and immediately
> on the Sabbath He entered the synagogue and
> began to teach. (v. 21)

After that, He went for lunch at Simon and Andrew's place along with friends. It turns out that Simon's mother-in-law was sick, so—as it would—the conversation turned toward her illness. Lucky for her, Jesus was in a healing mood and healed her and then she waited on them—hopefully with a yummy Sunday quiche or bubbling mimosas.

> *You don't see Jesus complaining about all the people He had to talk with, counsel, attend to, or even work with. He lived life fully, extending His borders wide.*

Well, wouldn't you know after a few hours passed, people heard about Jesus's morning synagogue visit and lunch at Simon and Andrew's place, so they began bringing their friends who needed help to an impromptu healing party at the house.

> And immediately after they came out of the synagogue, they came into the house of Simon and Andrew, with James and John. Now Simon's mother-in-law was lying sick with a fever; and immediately they spoke to Jesus about her. And He came to her and raised her up, taking her by the hand, and the fever left her, and she waited on them.
>
> When evening came, after the sun had set, they began bringing to Him all who were ill and those who were demon-possessed. And the whole city had gathered at the door.
>
> (Mark 1:29-32 NASB)

This all happened on the Sabbath—His day *off*.

Clearly, all of this interrupted the Sunday afternoon football games and naps.

He was busy—preaching here, healing there—but it would be more accurate to say that His life was full.

On a day with no agenda, His day was full of people. More people than usual. More teaching. More healing. More life-giving instances. It wasn't work to Him. It was His pleasure to do it, or He wouldn't have done it. Plain and simple.

We need more of this. More pleasure in His will, so that we can get more of Him. These things that bog us down, what takes effort, what needs us—they need a holy filter covering them in order for Jesus to infiltrate our minds and hearts.

With a whole and holy perspective on every single thing we come across, our lives will continually build into one like Jesus's.

You don't see Jesus complaining about all the people He had to talk with, counsel, attend to, or even work with. He lived life fully, extending His borders wide. He didn't worry about where His next meal or bed would come from. He did what the Father called him to do, as He said in Mark 1:38, "That is why I have come."

He was the first WHOLE and HOLY person who showed us the way.

So what happens when we believe God for more?

Jesus happens.

*Being spiritually paralyzed often feels like Jesus is off teaching everybody else and has forgotten about us in our mounds of dirty diapers, endless laundry, and slippery emotions.*

Specifically believing for more of Him in the life He wants us to have. We only get this life by getting more of Jesus.

When we believe Jesus for more, He gives us more—of Himself. He is the way to more life.

But it's not easy. Though it is simple. We just need to make sure we overcome any paralysis we may face in grabbing hold of Him.

## Spiritual Paralysis

I've heard that the average person will see approximately five thousand messages a day, and those messages pertain just to active marketing. The marketing world calls this "noise."

And this noise crowds our life.

Marketing messages don't include our other things like needy toddlers, work emails, sick parents, PTO meetings, soccer and gymnastics practice, small group dinners, doctor appointments, grocery store runs, homework, and so on. Our lives are filled with all kinds of noise.

Want to know something scary? These things are all good (well, some of them), but too much of them can lead to what I call spiritual paralysis. That is when our soul—the part of us directly connected to God—is unable to function.

Being spiritually paralyzed often feels like Jesus is off teaching everybody else, along on someone else's wildly fabulous spiritual journey, and has forgotten about us in our mounds of dirty diapers, endless laundry, and slippery emotions.

Everyone else has stories of what He's done recently for them, how they've felt His presence, or what He's told them. They can see, feel, and hear Him, but it feels like He's not with us.

Worse yet, spiritual paralysis may even mean not seeing Him at all, anywhere.

It is often knowing He's near or taking care of things, but we're not a part of it, necessarily. Have you been through a time when you've felt disconnected from Him? Do you feel that way now?

There's something I can promise you when it comes to living this life, living our whole and holy lives Jesus has offered. We *will* go through seasons of spiritual paralysis. Even if we've been Christians for longer than we can remember. Even if we attend church, read our Bible regularly, or even preach Jesus to others in our lives.

It's just the way it is on this side of heaven. Until we are kicking it with the angels and saints at the feet of Jesus, there will be some level of disconnect.

Whether that's just the regular static between heaven and earth due to long distance, or whether it's a lack of frequency going up or coming down on our behalf, it will happen.

It will happen as we go about our day. It can even happen while we pray and worship.

I can almost hear some people clucking their tongues at me now. "Doesn't this contradict what the Bible tells us?" they're asking quietly, trying to steer me back on the straight and narrow. "The Bible says that Jesus is always 'there' and always with us."

Yes, dear friends, you're right. Jesus *is* with us.

He's in our midst. I mean, His name—Emmanuel—literally means "God with us."

But I venture to say that sometimes we need to go find Him. We need to find Him and look Him dead in the eyes.

But sometimes it's hard to see Jesus right next to us.

Just because we know somebody is near doesn't mean we always see them, hear them, or feel them. So sometimes we need to look for Him to get more of Him.

And the absolute best time to seek Jesus is in the middle of life, in the middle of the mess.

Recently, I noticed I was beginning the traumatic shift from feeling spiritually stable to spiritually anemic.

Toward the end of the school semester, life at my house got really busy, really quickly. The kids needed me more than normal, my friends' schedules cleared up and they wanted to do things together, and family decided to travel in from out of town. All this came on top of work deadlines, bills, and regular busy life.

Life became overwhelming, and I could barely keep up with it. I knew I'd never make it through the coming weeks without letting the kids drive me crazy or screaming at everyone in sight.

> *Satan tried to use the chaos in my life to rock my tiny little world, but Jesus used it to stabilize me in His world. I'd been so distracted, side-eyeing these situations as roadblocks instead of road signs, that I'd lost my connection with Him.*

Because I was busy and overwhelmed, I knew things couldn't continue like they were. Life was coming at me so fast I couldn't feel or hear Jesus, and before it knocked me over, I needed to change something.

I needed to flip the narrative.

I wasn't just a bystander watching the parade of my day-to-day race on by. I needed to remember I was a part of this parade and those busy details were happening for my benefit. I needed to stop thinking life was happening *to* me. Instead it was happening *for* me.

Just as Jesus doesn't just happen to me; He happens for me.

And it's still like that now. For all of us.

These busy days, my work performance appraisal, sick kids, end-of-the-year teacher gifts and school madness, and yes, even the overnight trip to the trauma ER after Bryant's cycling accident a few weeks ago haven't happened *to* me just to try and take me out. They happened *for* me.

Jesus gifted me these so I could experience Him more. Sure, Satan tried to use them to rock my tiny little world, but Jesus offered them to me to stabilize me in His world.

But I'd been so distracted, side-eyeing these situations as roadblocks instead of road signs, that I'd lost my connection with Him. I lost sight of what He wanted to give me and do for me.

I'd been so focused on how to keep things moving in my world, I drifted slowly from Him. That drift led me to the initial tingles of spiritual paralysis.

So what do we do to connect or reconnect to get more from Jesus? We get creative.

## It's Time to Get Creative

The Bible tells a story of a paralyzed man's friends taking him to Jesus in Luke 5. Well, technically, I'm not sure if these guys were the man's friends, but based on the story and what they did, we're going to assume they were the best kind of friends.

Do you remember this story? In case you need a reminder, here's the gist.

Some dude isn't able to walk—totally paralyzed—and four of his friends decide they need to take him to a healer man who's come back in town. This paralyzed man is bedridden, so they carry him *and* his bed to the house Jesus is visiting.

Because Jesus is the BMC (Big Man on Campus, or in this case

Big Man in Capernaum), He's surrounded by people and the house He teaches in is overflowing. So much so that there isn't any room to get through the door or windows. I imagine people are squatting, standing, sitting, pushing through the doors, and hanging in the open windows to hear what Jesus has to say.

These friends couldn't get the bed through the door or the windows due to all the people. So they climbed up on top of the house, removed roof tiles, and lowered the man down right in front of Jesus.

And then, to wrap up the story nice and neat, the Hero (that's Jesus) saw their faith, forgave the paralyzed man's sins, and healed the man so he could walk again.

Because *of course* He did.

There's the story.

There are a few points I feel are good for us to visit.

Let's start with Luke 5:18-19. Here, the friends carrying their friend remind me of me.

> "They were seeking to bring him in and lay him
> before Jesus, but *finding no way* to bring him in,
> *because of the crowd*" (Luke 5:18-19, emphasis mine)

Sometimes I can't find a way to Jesus.

I try and try, but I can't. We chatted about this already when discussing our quiet times, but as a reminder, a few examples for me are:

- I set my alarm earlier, and my kids get up earlier.
- I change my quiet time from morning to right before bed, and I am so tired I fall asleep.
- I choose a time during the day I know will be quiet without kids, but then an unexpected visitor shows up.

So on and so on . . . and so on.

Sometimes the crowd—the kids, our schedules, our feelings, other obligations—get in our way of seeing Him.

*The Message* version of Luke 5:18-20 reads:

> They went up on the roof, removed some tiles,
> and let him down in the *middle of everyone*, right
> in front of Jesus. (emphasis mine)

In the middle of the mess, they placed their mess in front of Jesus. And how'd they do it? They went up on the roof and removed tiles. Who does that? My neighbors would freak their freak if I climbed up on their roof, let alone destroyed the tiles while up there. All in the name of Jesus.

*God will see your faith, where your heart is rooted, and heal your paralysis.*

These dudes did something they knew could (and probably would) have repercussions.

They were creative and bold in their strategy to be with Jesus, to heal the paralysis. And guess what? It worked.

> Impressed by their bold belief, he said, "Friend,
> I forgive your sins." (Luke 5:20)

Sometimes we have to be creative to be with our Creator.

And that's what I want to encourage you to do. Today. Right now. In thirty minutes, in three hours, and in three months.

Do something bold.
Do something creative.
Do something that isn't "normal" to be with your God.

Maybe this means you hire a babysitter, like I did, and go for a long walk around the neighborhood with your audiobook Bible and some headphones. Maybe you, like me, can't justify spending the money for an hourlong walk, but you do it anyway. Maybe this becomes a weekly routine.

Maybe this means spending fifteen minutes sitting in your car in the school parking lot after drop-off or even locked in a quiet bathroom reading God's Word. Let everyone wonder what you're doing in there. Who cares?

Maybe this means literally listing every single strained feeling, irritation, desire, or need on a sheet of paper and then lighting that sheet on fire as you ask God to take them away.

Does that last one seem a little too pyromaniacal to you? Who cares? If it works, it works.

Whatever it is, do it. Think outside the proverbial Jesus box. Because God will see your faith, where your heart is rooted, and heal your paralysis. Every. Time.

And maybe—hopefully—we won't have to remove our neighbor's roof.

## Less Is More

OK, so lighting our scribbled notes on fire may seem a little extreme as a way to get more of Jesus, but you can't hate on the brainstorming. Not only is creativity necessary sometimes, but I believe God celebrates it in us.

However, if you're more of a rule-following soul than an arsonist, I've got an even better solution for you in finding more life through Jesus.

There are two things that will give us more of Jesus.

Just two. And they are nonnegotiable.

First Timothy 2:8 says that in every place men (and women)

should pray, and John 8:31 tells us of when Jesus told the Jews who believed in him, "If you abide in my word, you are truly my disciples."

We must pray and read His Word.

I know what you're thinking—duh. *Of course* we have to pray and read about Him. Simple enough, right?

Then why is this so hard for so many of us?

Why is prayer a last resort instead of our knee-jerk reaction? And why do our Bibles get dusty on our bedsides?

> *The goal of prayer shouldn't be to sound more spiritual and wise but to become more spiritual and wise.*

What if we simplify it even more? What if we take out a step and lessen our load?

Can we through simplifying become powerful? And more whole and holy in the process?

Instead of praying *and* reading His Word, let's *pray His Word.*

Take His words from the Bible, and pray them right back to Him.

Before I go on, I need you to know the last thing I want you to think is that I'm a great example for you in this department.

Nope. Not at all.

I make mistakes in prayer, and just like in my walk of faith, I am still learning what God has to teach me. However, I've drawn inspiration from many books on prayer, as well as from my friend Emily.

Emily is a total prayer warrior for her kiddos and family, and it's inspiring. It's not a new concept, but one I didn't really put together until I saw Emily do it. It's brilliant, and yet so simple.

So I wanted to let you know the same battle weapon for prayer that Emily, myself, and . . . oh yeah, *Jesus* . . . have is also available to you.

As Christians, we believe prayer is important, but we also must know that praying Scripture is powerful.

First of all, you'll sound super smart and spiritual.

Just kidding.

The goal of prayer shouldn't be to sound more spiritual and wise (even though that's fun). The goal of prayer is to become more spiritual and wise.

I'm not one who uses eloquent and profound words, and I have been known to fumble and bumble over many a prayer. Even many regular conversations. Maybe you're like me too.

However, God is eloquent and profound. His Word has all the profoundness needed in this world written out in plain English for us. When it comes to wisdom and eloquence, God trumps all.

So why does this even matter?

To be "eloquent" means to clearly express something or be persuasive in what you speak or write. Our prayers have a powerful impact not only on our future but also on our faith. They are persuasive, especially with the Holy Spirit bidding on our behalf like it says in Romans 8.

> Likewise the Spirit helps us in our weakness. For
> we do not know what to pray for as we ought,
> but the Spirit himself intercedes for us with
> groanings too deep for words. (v. 26)

Using God's clearly expressed and persuasive words, His own words, we have an impact on everything—a powerful impact.

This was God's plan all along—that we engage with Him. He loves it, so He gave us perfect and wise words to pray to and with Him so that we pray within God's will.

God's Word says so right here in 1 John 5:14-15:

> This is the confidence we have in approaching
> God: that if we ask anything according to his
> will, he hears us. And if we know that he hears
> us—whatever we ask—we know that we have
> what we asked of him. (NIV)

All through the Bible we find God's will for people, for you and for me. It's literally written in there. So we need to ask for what He wants for us too, because then it is certain—certain!—to happen.

> You ask and do not receive, because you ask
> wrongly, to spend it on your passions. (James 4:3)

Every time we choose to think Christ's thoughts and speak God's Word instead of our own, we are training ourselves to transform our way of thinking (Romans 12:2) into His way of thinking and, therefore, adopting His will for us.

So let's pray His Word.

And just like that, we've simplified our two steps to receiving more of God into one. One thing we can do throughout our days to bring more of Jesus into the daily grind.

When praying Scripture becomes a habit throughout more of our day, it changes our perspective on everything. It changes how we see life—our life.

We filter everything through a Scripture-based, godly perspective. A whole and holy perspective.

Did you know filters on film cameras are used to protect the front of a lens from harsh, invisible light? It ultimately keeps the light from damaging the inner film.

What if our Scripture-based prayers do the same? What if they protect us and our minds from harsh, invisible forces that try to destroy our wholeness and holiness?

Wow—praise God.

## A Quick, Final, and Insanely Incredible Reminder

Friend, these pages have been a labor of love for me. But I think I owe you a reminder that I—as you've seen through these pages—do not have this whole thing figured out.

I also owe it to you to remind you of where we started this whole conversation.

Living whole and holy is not just up to you.

Just like it's not up to me.

Jesus provides the means and the motivation, no matter where, how, or when we work, no matter how our children turn out or where we will be the next year or down the road.

His whole life and His holy life must become more of ours if we are to be whole and holy as well.

The thing—the *only* thing—we have to do is believe that what He set out to do is done.

His wholeness and His holiness take the place of ours. Because of this salvation of ours, our lives are whole and complete, holy and set apart from the world we live in.

**This life—because of Jesus—doesn't need more *from* moms. It gives more *for* moms.**

More Jesus. More love. More life.

As loving, busy, work-hard mamas, we know life can beat us down and take from us.

But it's a lie that we have to give so much that we are depleted emotionally, physically, and spiritually every day. Even when it doesn't feel like it, we know we live in a place of abundance, a place of wholeness and holiness through our Christ Jesus.

We know wholeness is how we were created and is our natural state. We know holiness is what God has clothed us in through the death and resurrection of His Son. We know that His timeless spiritual disciplines (fasting, prayer, and prioritizing time for Him) aren't just feel-good options to fix our problems, but *holy* means to place us—our minds and our lives—in a more humble and correct position under the authority of almighty God.

Only when we live strong in faith of our whole and holy lives do we get to receive more. It's when we accept Christ as the means to whole and holy. It's when we accept and daily remind ourselves of our faith in what He's done.

**And we're there, my friend. We're already there—whole and holy.**

It's more than we can *even begin* to imagine before we see our Jesus face-to-face.

And all the tired—yet utterly joyful—mamas said AMEN.

# Invitation to Be Whole and Holy

Dear friend, I need you to know that I wrote this book with the woman in mind who already believes Christ to be her Lord and Savior. BUT (and this is a big "but") . . .

*That doesn't mean these words don't apply if you don't yet have a relationship with Christ.*

Whether you consider yourself a Christian or not, the reality is that we have an enemy who schemes against us, seeking to steal, kill, and destroy (see 2 Corinthians 2:11 and John 10:10).

We can see the results of this enemy's work everywhere. Just turn on the news.

But we can also see the work of our Savior. He's a Savior who stands for everything the enemy will not and cannot. A Savior who is for us and works all things together for the good of those who love Him and are called according to His purpose (Romans 8:28). A Savior who wants us to be with Him. Lucky for us, He always has our best interests at heart.

I feel I would be doing you a disservice if I didn't allow you an opportunity and a spot in these pages to accept Christ into your life. If you have been wondering what this Christian thing looks and feels like, and whenever you are ready for Jesus in your life, then pray with me the prayer at the end of this section. You don't have to have a super profound-ish spiritual moment right now to do it either.

Simply ask yourself if you believe Jesus Christ is the Son of God, that He died and was resurrected in order to save His people. If you believe this—make the *choice* to believe this—then I'm doing a jig in my seat for you right now (along with a thousand angels in heaven)!

I tend to be pretty heavy on Scripture application in my life, and I've done the same in this book, so I hope reading this book has helped you in your understanding of what a Christ-led life looks like. It's not perfect, but it is set apart and whole.

What you read may have hurt you, made you angry, or felt like a sucker punch. Or maybe it made you laugh or smile knowingly.

Whatever reactions you may be having after reading these chapters are likely a response to how the Holy Spirit is working within you. The Holy Spirit helps us hear God through His Word, and my intent in writing this book was to base it firmly upon God's Word—saturating it with Scripture and truth. I prayed over every sentence, and it is my prayer that the Holy Spirit will help you hear exactly what you need to hear as you read.

I know these thoughts and feelings are from Him because He's made me feel all the same feelings you may experience. The things I write and share in here that He's taught me have made me mad, hurt my feelings, and made me jump for joy—sometimes simultaneously.

My prayer is that you and everyone who reads this book come to know Jesus and His love for you—for us—just a tiny bit better.

Because He's got more in mind for us, Mama. He's just waiting for you and me to grab ahold of it. Our whole-and-holy mom lives are waiting for us to live.

Much love,
Kristin

If you openly declare that Jesus is Lord and believe in your heart that God raised him from the dead, you will be saved. For it is by believing in your heart that you are made right with God, and it is by openly declaring your faith that you are saved. (Romans 10:9-10 NLT)

## Pray This Prayer of Salvation

Jesus, thank You for loving me and for dying for me on the cross. I understand and believe You are my Lord and my Savior, now and for all eternity. I know if I confess with my mouth and believe in my heart that You raised your Son, Jesus, from the dead, I will be saved. Father, I confess my sin and believe that now. I offer my life to You and believe You died as a sacrifice for my sin, Your blood washing me clean, and then rose victoriously from the grave and are living today. Because of You, I am a child of God and heaven is my final destination and home. Send Your Holy Spirit into me, and may I walk by the Spirit all the rest of my days. Thank You for the work You have done and the work You will continue to do in my life. In the precious and holy name of Jesus Christ. Amen.

# Acknowledgments

I couldn't start the acknowledgements section without first mentioning my Prayer Team Warriors: Mary Ann, Abby, Amy, Phyllis, Jill, and Emily. This project only came to be because of your intercession. I know and feel that to the core of my bones. I love each of you so very much.

Launch Team! Y'all are the best. This book is out there being shared in the world because of you. *Thank you.*

To everyone who stepped in to help watch, feed, and play with my crazy kiddos while I disappeared to write these words down, your energy and love for my kids does not go unappreciated.

Kimberly, your direction in understanding and conveying the message of God's Word was *such a blessing* to me. Thank you for your friendship and wisdom. Emily, my think tank, I'm so blessed to have you in my corner (jumping up and down clapping) cheering me on! To Ashley, the Voxer Queen, thank you for being a holy example of what motherhood in ministry looks like.

To my supper club wives, I love you girls and your families so big. Molly, my sister-wife, I'm so blessed to share this cycling and

BPC life with you. I wouldn't want to share the burden and blessing of parenting, plant obsession, or our boys' adventures with anyone else. Elizabeth, I can always count on you to bring a smile to my face. Your genuineness and zeal in the everyday challenges me in my own daily routine. I thought of you often as I wrote this book. Kelly, as we walked laps around the Lenox office during lunch one day, you were the very first person who ever told me I should write a book. Thank you for planting that seed in my heart. Lacey, you inspire me and challenge me to think beyond my small, suburban life. Thank you for being a cheerleader for me and opening my eyes to the bigger and more universal love of Jesus.

Freddie, your support of my writing and this project is unheard of for someone it has taken time and energy away from. Thank you for leading me and so many others well.

Wendy, look at you reading the acknowledgments! Thank you for ALL. THE. THINGS. Keeping me straight; reminding me where I have to be and when; reminding me who someone is; feeding me snacks; supporting and cheering for me, my family, and our brand of crazy.

My BDA gals, I'm so, so thankful for your friendship and guidance through this writers' journey.

Blythe, I praise God for you. Thank you for being the best champion for me and this message. You're more than the best agent out there. Your prayers, vision, guidance, and wisdom, not just for this project and publishing process but for me personally, shine like Jesus. I appreciate your friendship. I still remember the indescribable feeling when you first emailed me, as I nursed and rocked my last newborn. Thank you for catching and believing in me while I stumbled through the process of refining this project. I am a better writer because of you. I can't wait for our other adventures together!

Karen, Melissa, Sally, Elizabeth, Susan, Alison, and the rest of the team at Abingdon, picture me doing the MC Hammer happy dance right now. Because that's how pumped I am to have such an incredible team to package up and help put this message out into the world. This wannabe plant lady even got her very own succulents on the cover! #Spoiled Thank you for your enthusiasm and hard work in shaping this message for the rest of the world.

Mom, Dad, Katie, Storm, Rock, and Kathy, this life of following Christ is one of serving other people. I don't do that well. But I am so eternally grateful for having each of you as a daily reminder and example of how to love my people well. Dad, thank you for always being my biggest cheerleader. From day one. Rock and Kathy, thank you for loving me as your own and for loving on the littlest Funston girls as much as me. Storm, thank you for reading every word I wrote and being my very own personal English teacher. Not many people get to say their sister-in-law is one of their best friends. I'm so grateful. Katie, you've always been in my corner, cheering me on, getting my mind right, and standing up for me, even when we were acting like typical siblings. I love you so much. Mom, there are no words. I love you. Thank you. For everything.

McKenna, Meda, and Rockie May, you make me crazy, happy, joyful, and loved, but above all you make me better. Slowly and messily, but better nonetheless. I love you three to the moon and back. Forever and ever.

Bryant, here come the tears. No matter what I've ever wanted to do, you've been all in for me. Whether it was moving across the country for a job I always wanted, running a marathon I didn't think I could do, writing a blog post to share our lives with the internet, writing a book, or signing up to learn calligraphy (remember that waste of time and money?). You make me laugh when I want to scream, smile when I want to pout, stay quiet when I want to yell, and grow when I want to stay the same. You make me a better person. This book wouldn't have happened if it wasn't for you verbalizing your belief that I can do whatever I put my mind to. I love you.

My God. You split the sea so I could walk right through it. Thank You for letting me be a part of Your story.

CPSIA information can be obtained
at www.ICGtesting.com
Printed in the USA
LVHW012053020419
612742LV00002B/2